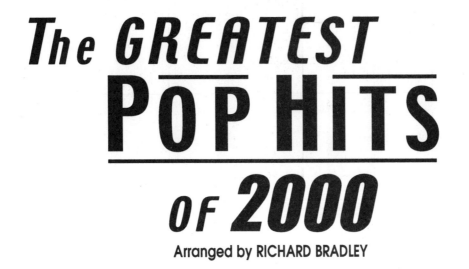

The GREATEST POP HITS OF 2000

Arranged by RICHARD BRADLEY

Project Manager: Carol Cuellar
Cover Design: Olivia D. Novak

CONTENTS

BYE BYE BYE

Words and Music by
KRISTIAN LUNDIN
JAKE and ANDREAS CARLSSON
Arranged by RICHARD BRADLEY

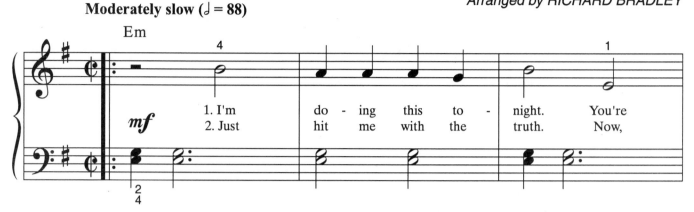

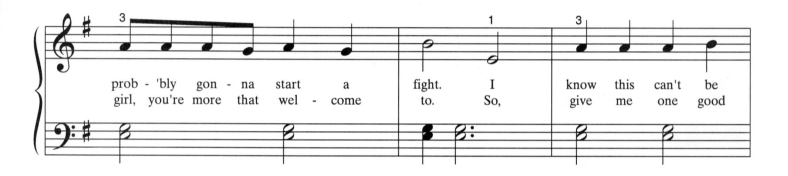

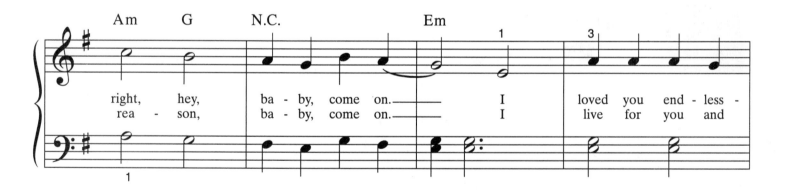

Bye Bye Bye - 5 - 1

4

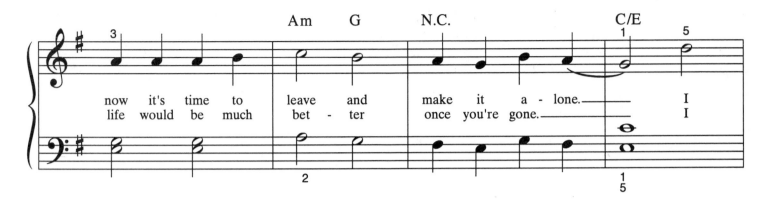

Am   G   N.C.   C/E

now it's time to leave and make it a - lone. _____ I
life would be much bet - ter once you're gone. _____ I

N.C.   C/E

know that I can't take no more. It ain't no lie. _____ I

N.C.

wan - na see you out that door. Ba - by, bye, bye, bye. _____

Em   D

I don't wan - na be a fool for you, _____ just an - oth - er play - er in your

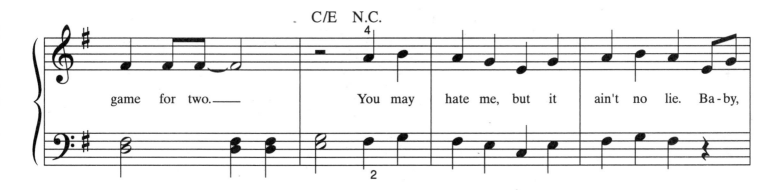

game for two.—

C/E   N.C.

You may hate me, but it ain't no lie. Ba-by,

Em

bye, bye, bye.— I don't real-ly wan-na make it tough,—

D

I just wan-na tell you that I had e-nough.—

C/E   N.C.

It may sound

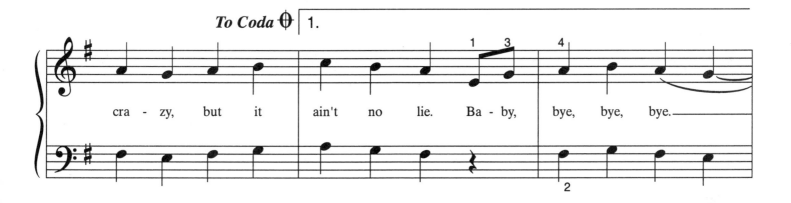

To Coda ⊕ | 1.

cra-zy, but it ain't no lie. Ba-by, bye, bye, bye.—

6

Bye Bye Bye - 5 - 4

7

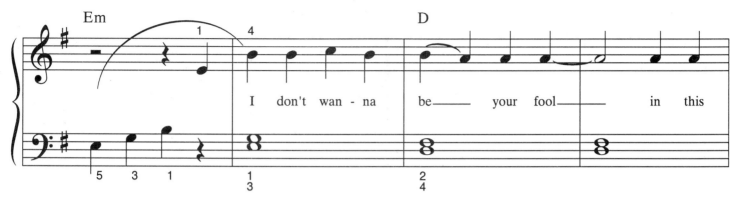

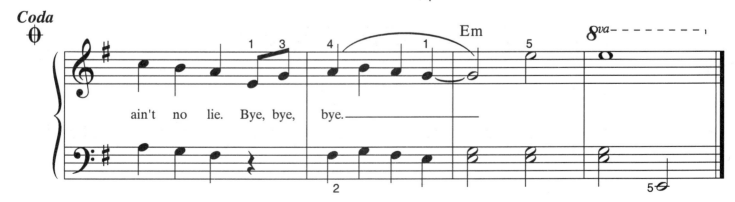

AMAZED

Words and Music by
MARV GREEN, AIMEE MAYO
and CHRIS LINDSEY
Arranged by RICHARD BRADLEY

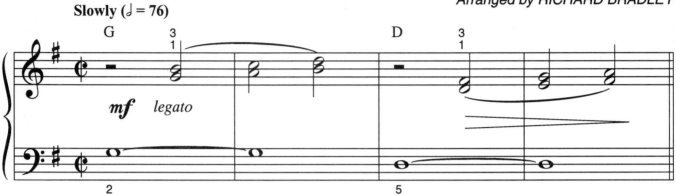

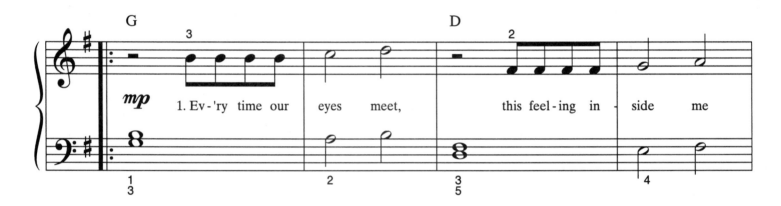

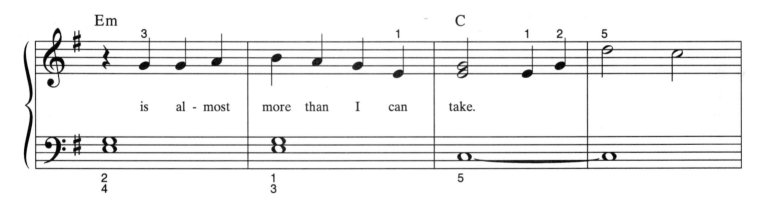

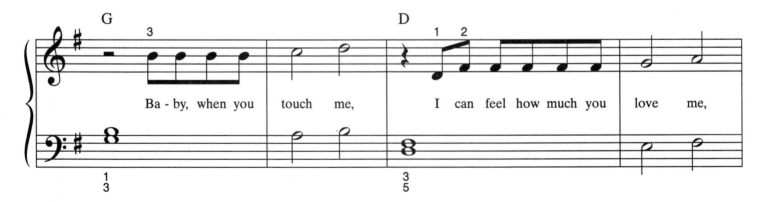

Amazed - 5 - 1

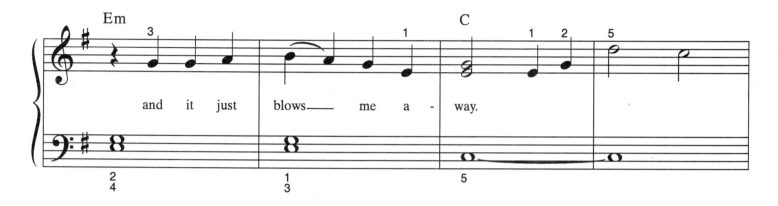

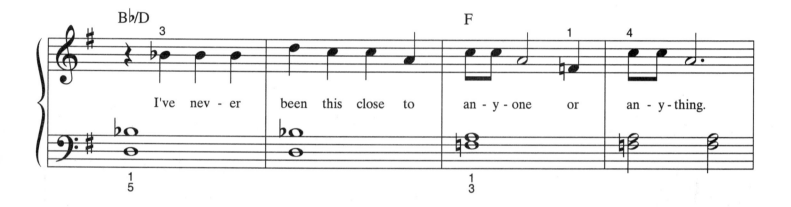

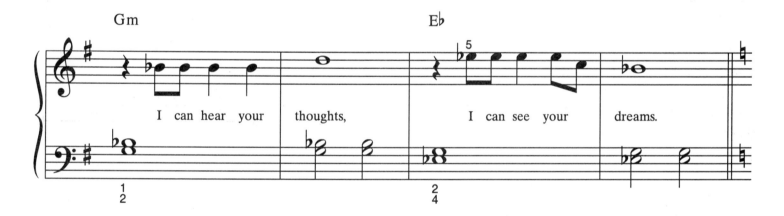

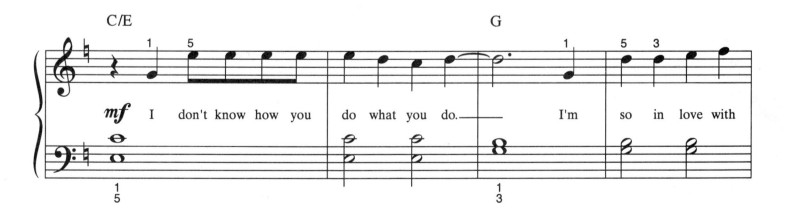

Amazed - 5 - 2

10

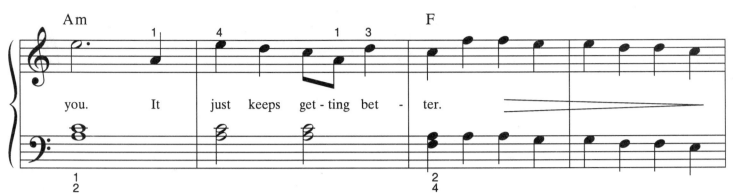

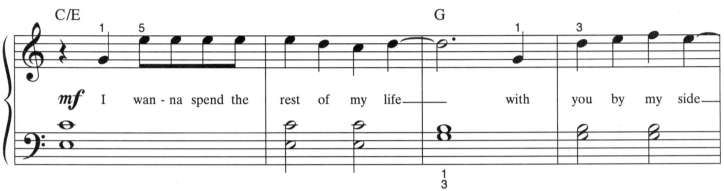

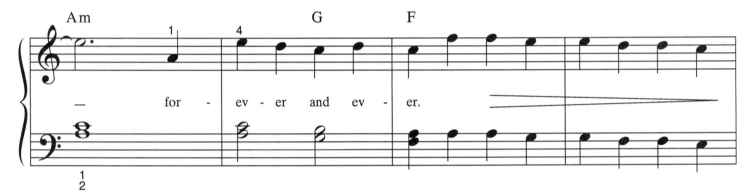

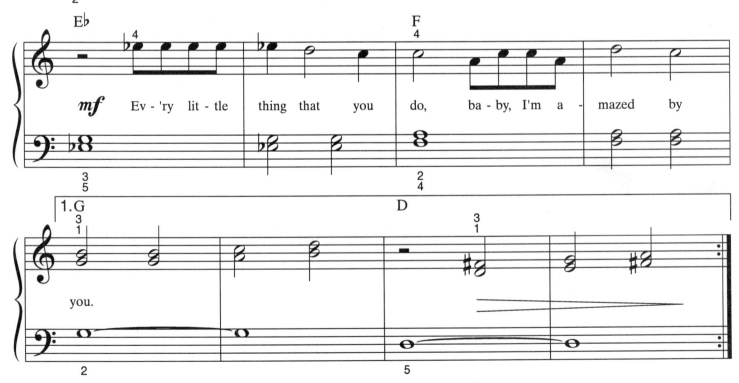

11

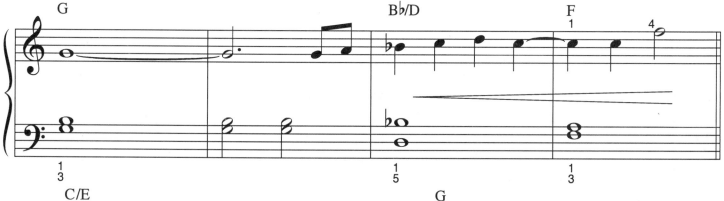

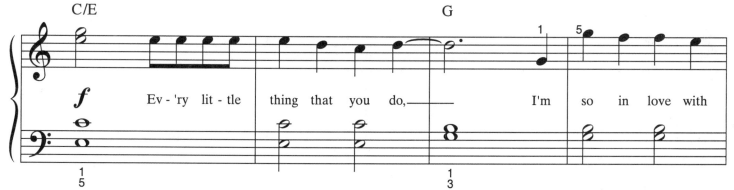

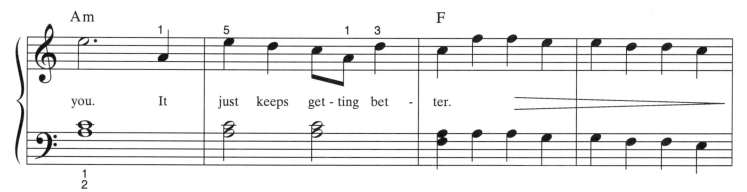

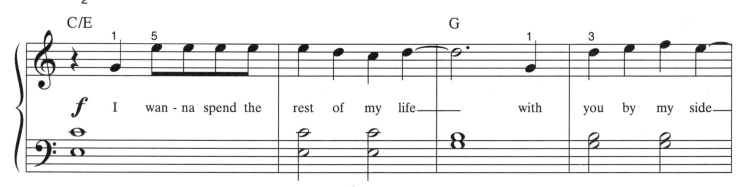

Amazed - 5 - 4

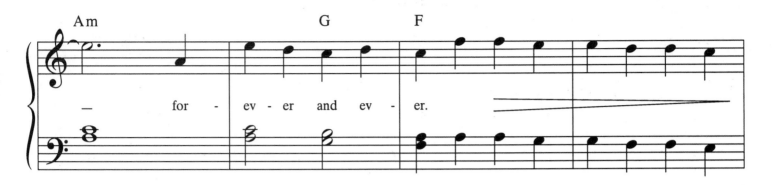

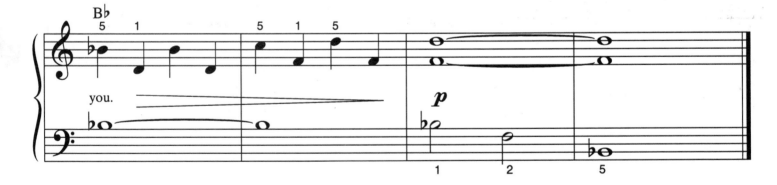

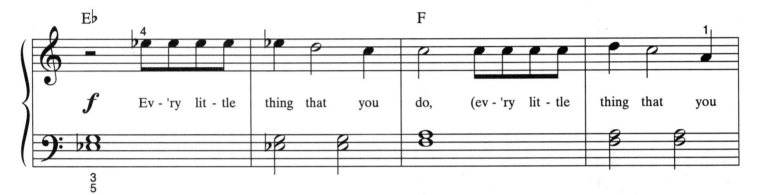

Verse 2:
The smell of your skin,
The taste of your kiss,
The way you whisper in the dark.
Your hair all around me,
Baby, you surround me.
You touch every place in my heart.
Oh, it feels like the first time every time.
I wanna spend the whole night in your eyes.
(To Chorus:)

AMERICAN PIE

Words and Music by
DON McLEAN
Arranged by RICHARD BRADLEY

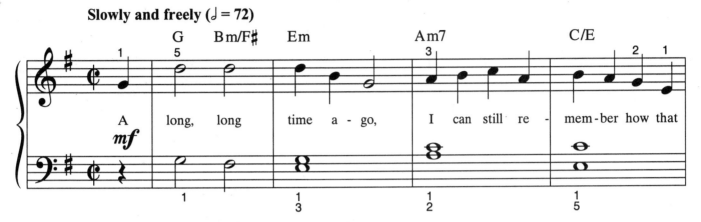

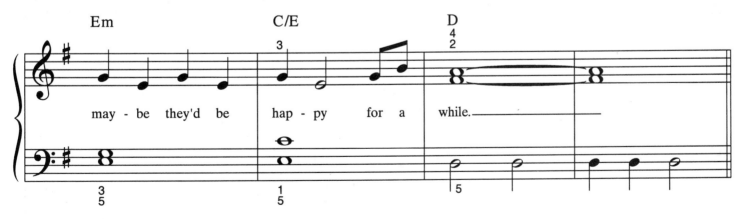

American Pie - 7 - 1

14

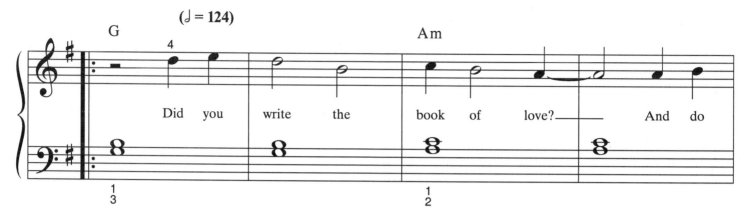

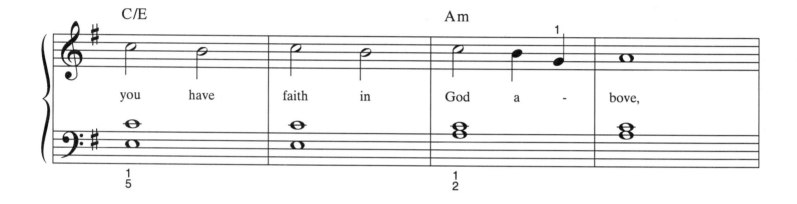

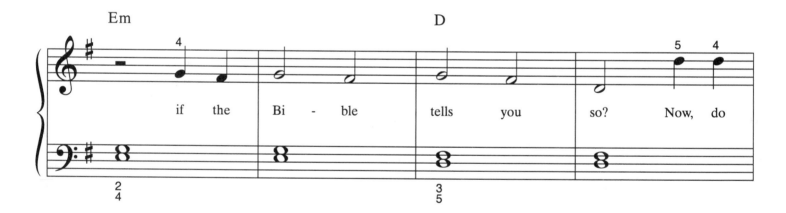

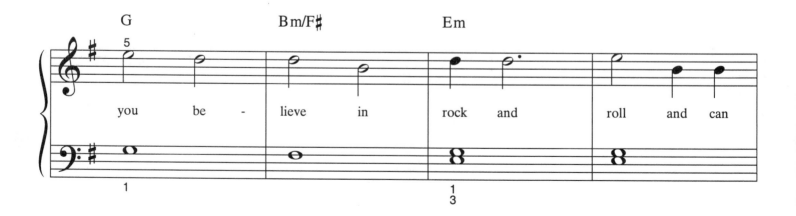

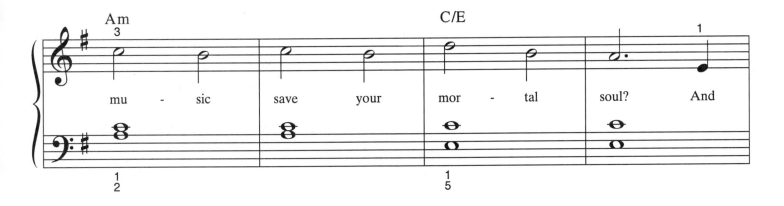

mu - sic   save   your   mor - tal   soul?   And

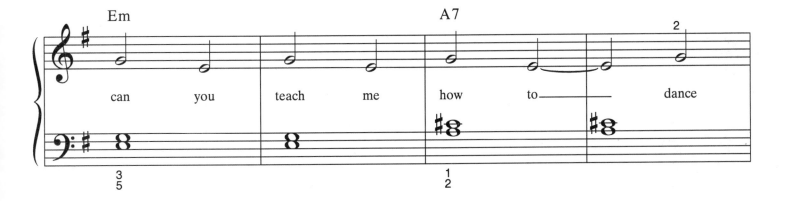

can   you   teach   me   how   to ——— dance

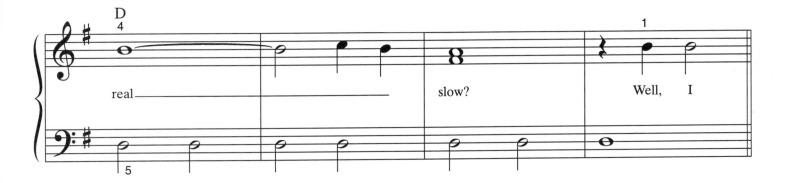

real ——————   slow?   Well,   I

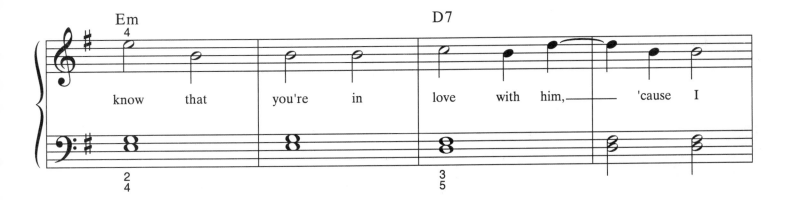

know   that   you're   in   love   with   him, ——   'cause   I

16

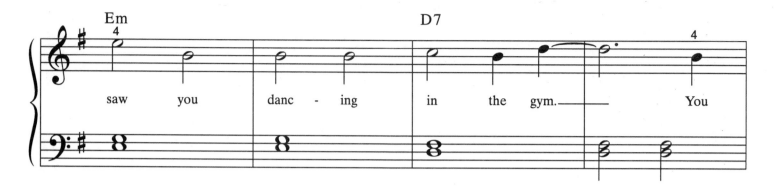

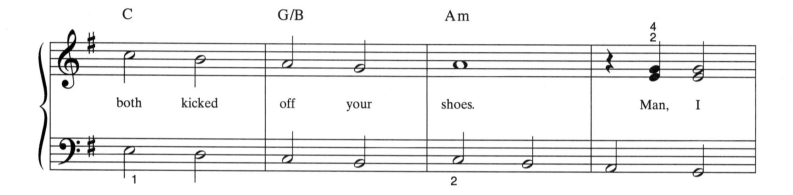

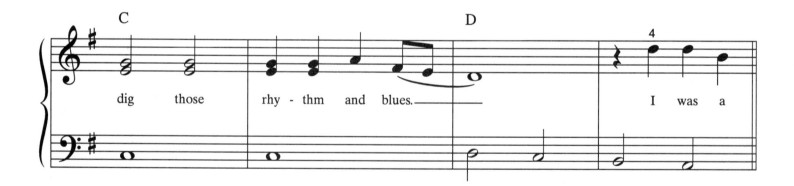

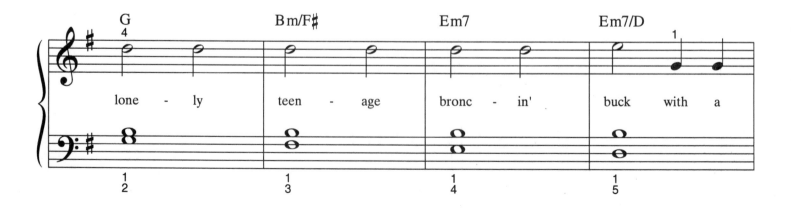

American Pie - 7 - 4

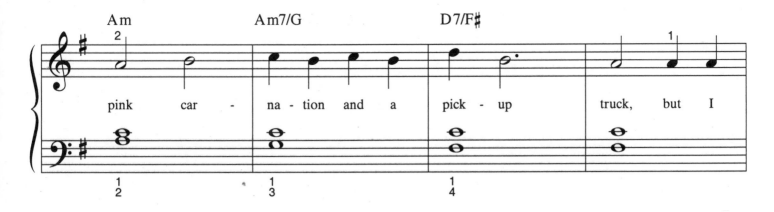

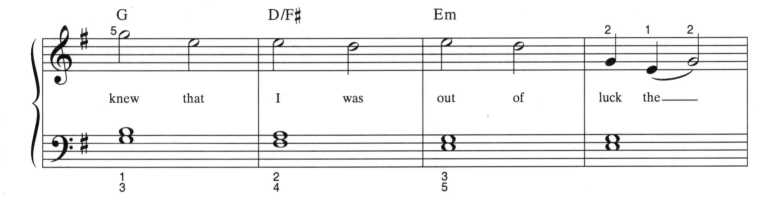

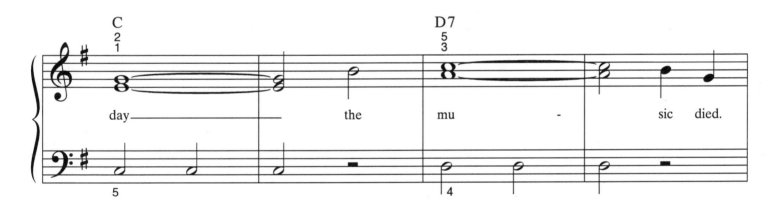

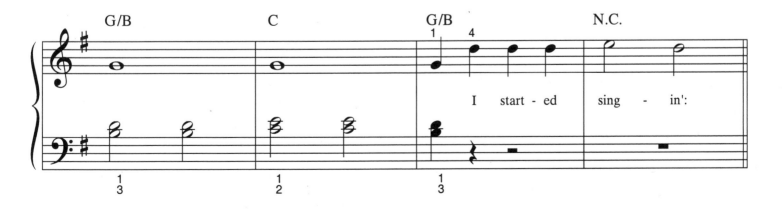

18

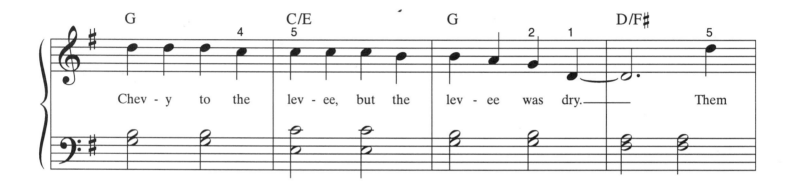

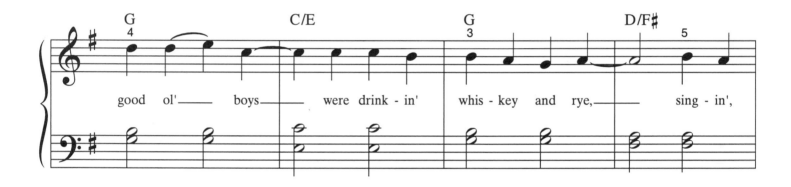

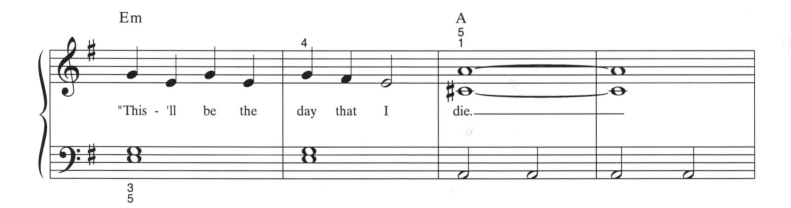

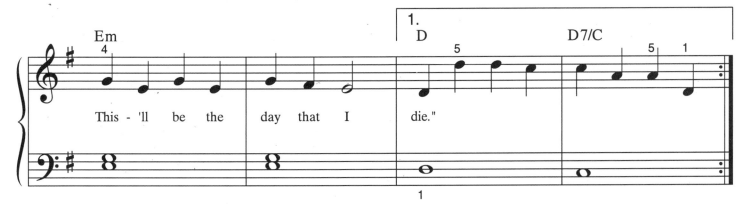

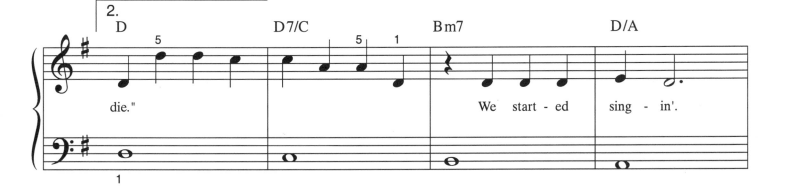

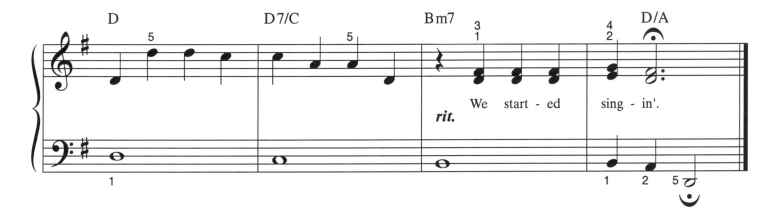

Verse 2:
I met a girl who sang the blues
And I asked her for some happy news,
But she just smiled and turned away.
I went down to the sacred store,
Where I heard the music years before,
But the man there said the music wouldn't play.
And in the streets, the children screamed,
The lovers cried and the poets dreamed.
But not a word was spoken;
The chuch bells were all broken.
And the three men I admire most,
The Father, Son and Holy Ghost,
They caught the last train for the coast
The day the music died.
And they were singin':
(To Chorus)

BACK AT ONE

Words and Music by
BRIAN McKNIGHT
Arranged by RICHARD BRADLEY

Slowly (♩ = 144)

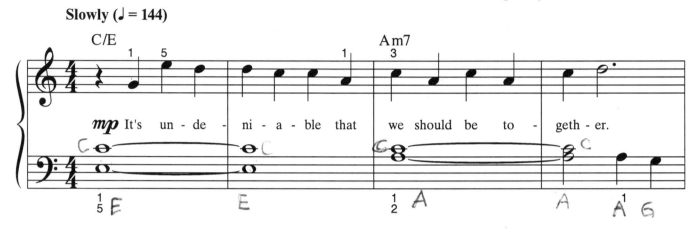

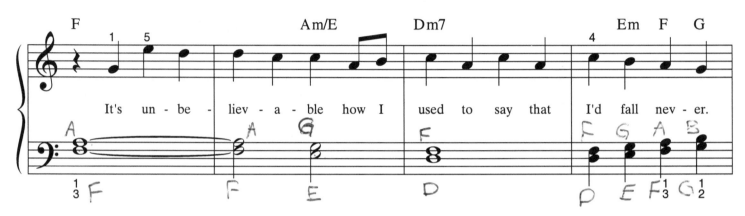

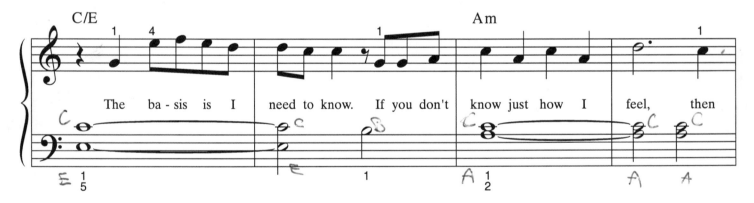

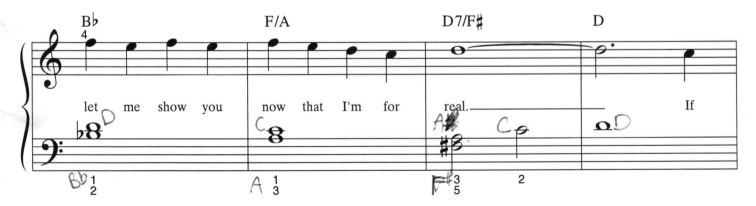

Back at One - 4 - 1

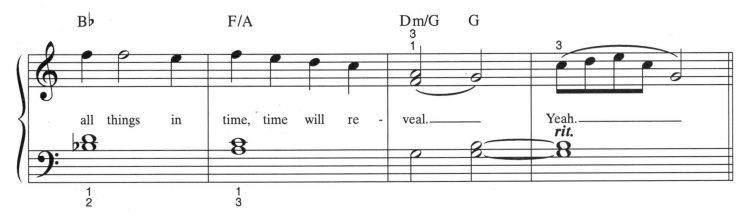

all things in time, time will re - veal._____ Yeah._____

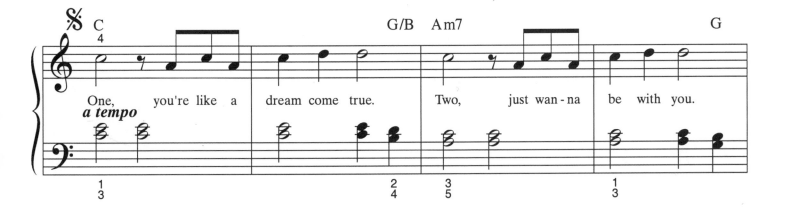

One, you're like a dream come true. Two, just wan-na be with you.

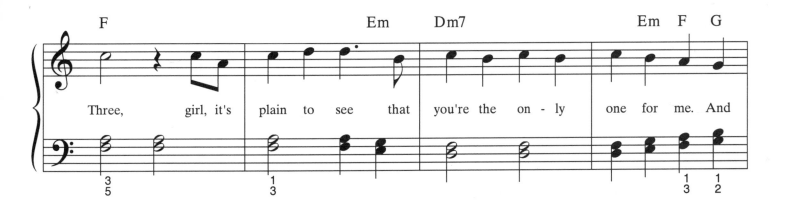

Three, girl, it's plain to see that you're the on - ly one for me. And

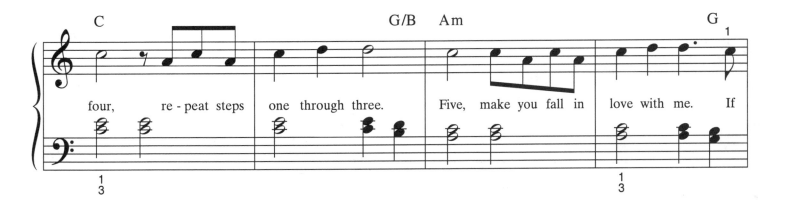

four, re-peat steps one through three. Five, make you fall in love with me. If

22

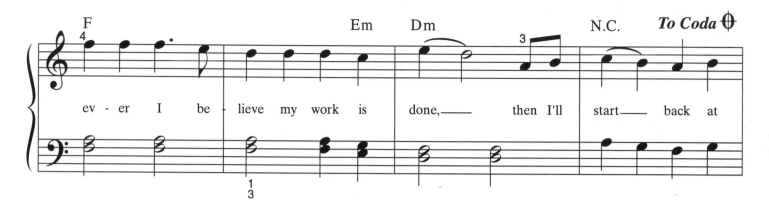

Back at One - 4 - 3

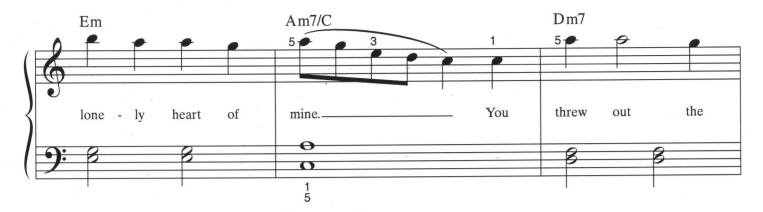

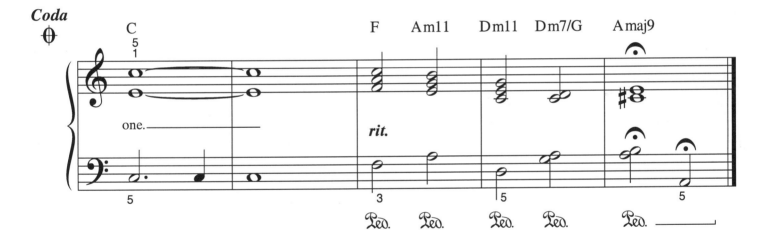

Verse 2:
It's so incredible, the way things work themselves out.
And all emotional, once you know what it's all about, hey.
And undesirable, for us to be apart.
I never would have made it very far,
'Cause you know you've got the keys to my heart.
'Cause one, you're like a dream come true.

CAN'T TAKE THAT AWAY
(MARIAH'S THEME)

Word and Music by
DIANE WARREN and
MARIAH CAREY
Arranged by RICHARD BRADLEY

Slowly (♩ = 52)

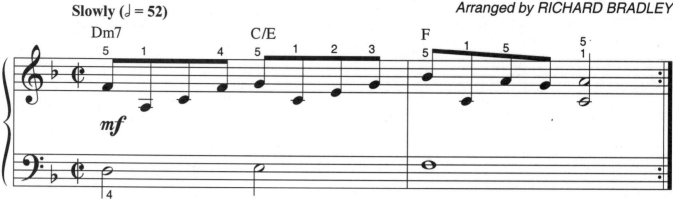

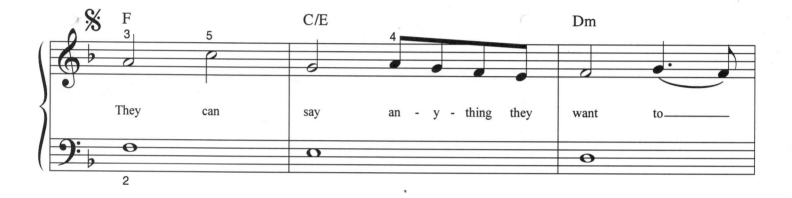

They can say an-y-thing they want to——

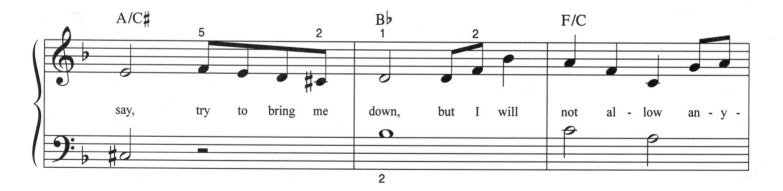

say, try to bring me down, but I will not al-low an-y-

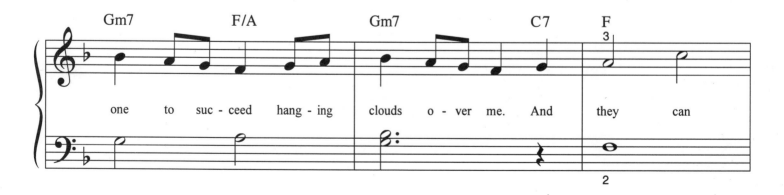

one to suc-ceed hang-ing clouds o-ver me. And they can

Can't Take That Away (Mariah's Theme) - 4 - 1

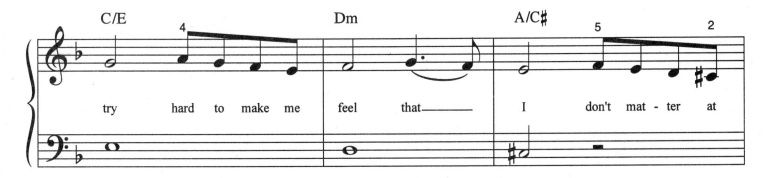

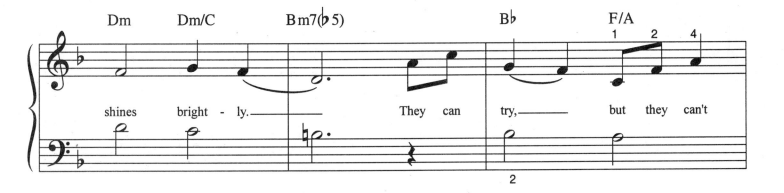

Can't Take That Away (Mariah's Theme) - 4 - 2

26

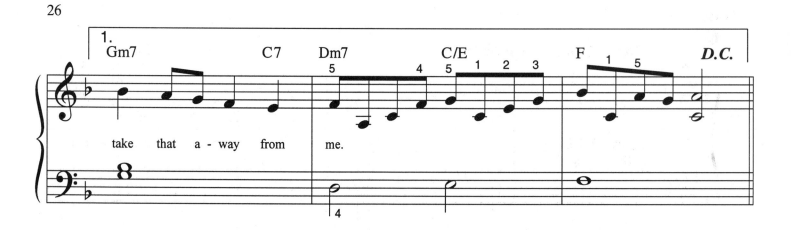

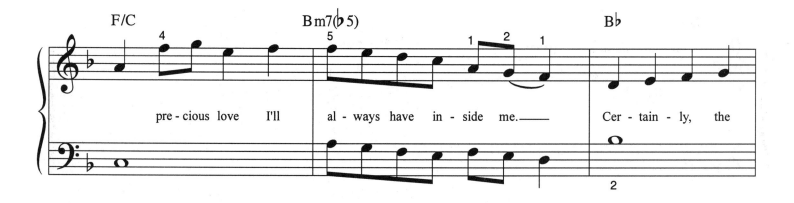

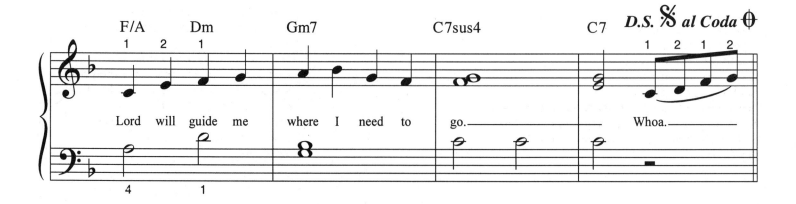

Can't Take That Away (Mariah's Theme) - 4 - 3

Coda

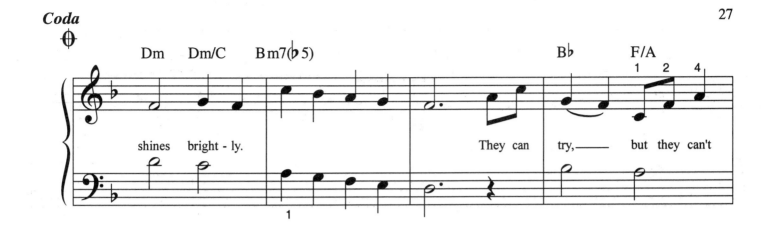

Dm Dm/C Bm7(♭5)   B♭ F/A

shines   bright - ly.   They can   try,—— but they can't

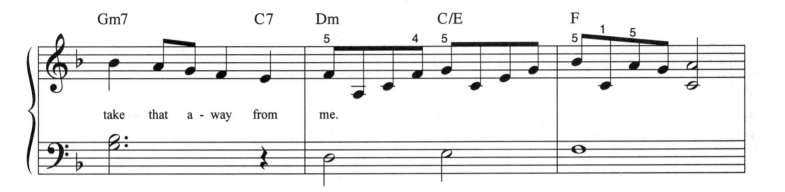

Gm7   C7   Dm   C/E   F

take   that   a - way   from   me.

Dm   C/E   F

rit.

Verse 2:
They can do anything they want to you
If you let them in.
But they won't ever win
If you cling to your pride
And just push them aside.
See, I have learned there's an inner peace I own.
Something in my soul that they cannot possess.
So I won't be afraid and darkness will fade.
(To Chorus:)

Verse 3 (sung an octave higher):
They can say anything they want to say,
Try to break me down,
But I won't face the ground.
I will rise steadily, sailing out of their reach.
Oh, Lord, they do try hard to make me feel
That I don't matter at all.
But I refuse to falter in what I believe
Or lose faith in my dreams.
(To Chorus:)

CANDY

Words and Music by
DENISE RICH, DAVE KATZ
and DENNY KLEIMAN
Arranged by RICHARD BRADLEY

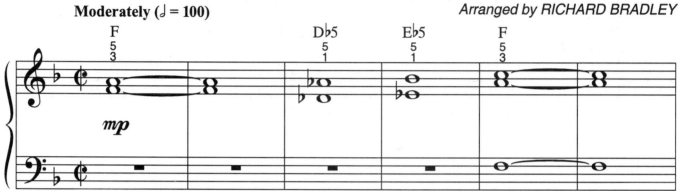

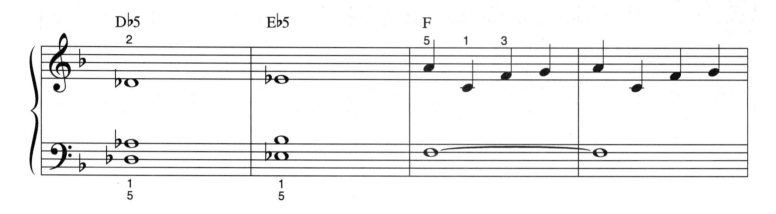

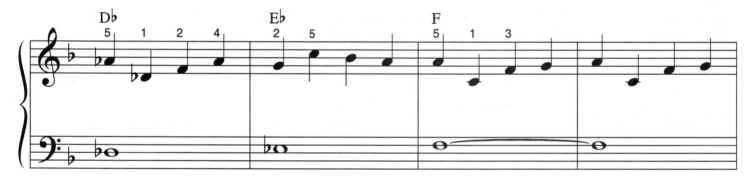

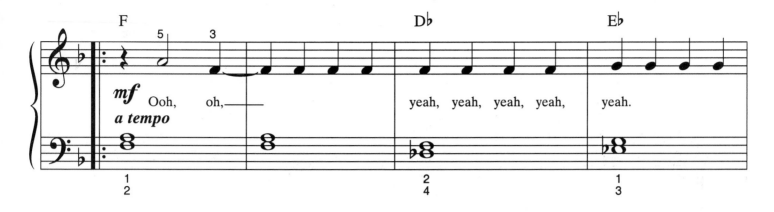

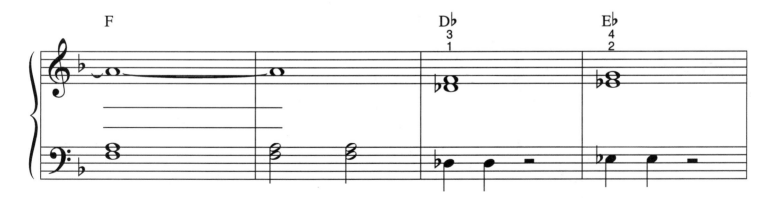

Candy - 6 - 2

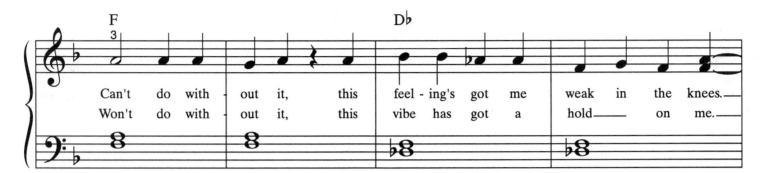

Can't do with - out it, this feel - ing's got me weak in the knees.
Won't do with - out it, this vibe has got a hold on me.

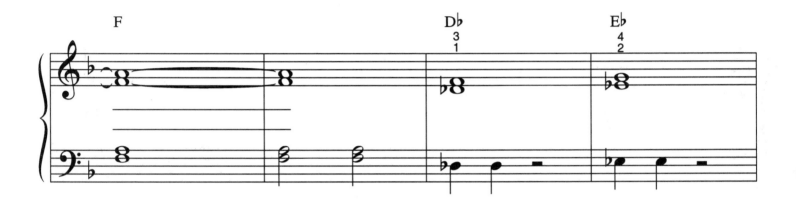

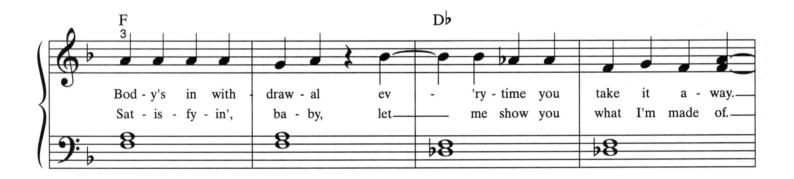

Bod - y's in with - draw - al ev - 'ry - time you take it a - way.
Sat - is - fy - in', ba - by, let me show you what I'm made of.

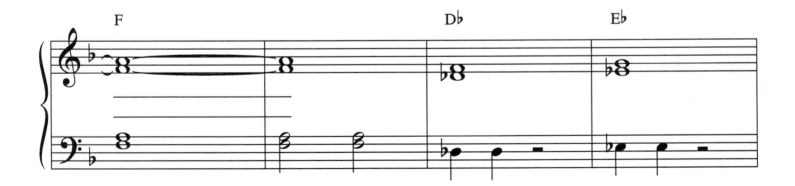

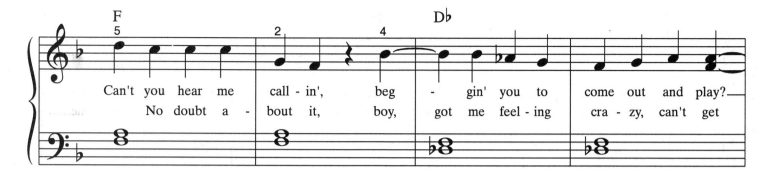

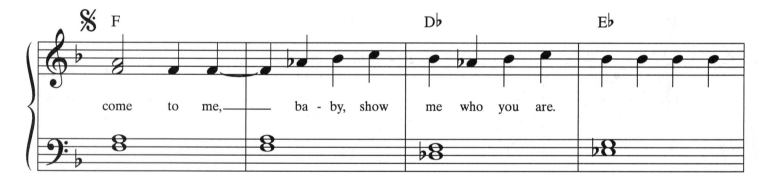

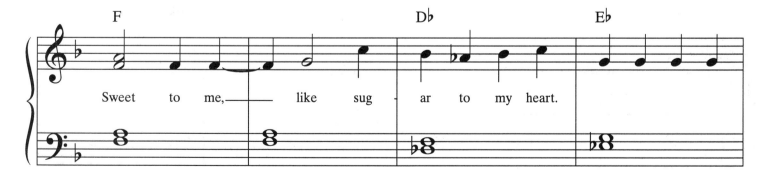

Candy - 6 - 4

32

I'm crav - ing for you. I'm miss - ing you___ like can -

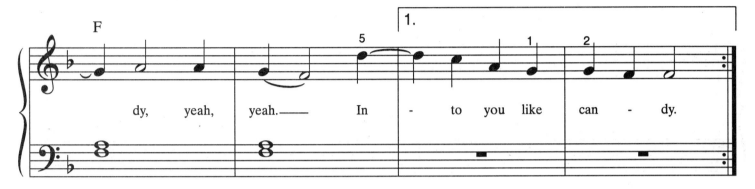

dy, yeah, yeah.___ In - to you like can - dy.

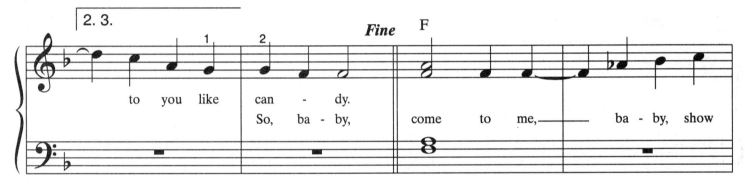

to you like can - dy.
So, ba - by, come to me,___ ba - by, show

me who you are. Sweet to me,___ like sug -

ar to my heart. I'm crav - ing for you.

33

I'm miss-ing you_ like can - dy, yeah, yeah._

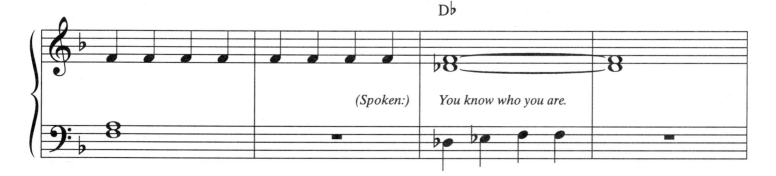

(Spoken:) You know who you are.

Your love's as sweet as candy.   I'll be forever yours.

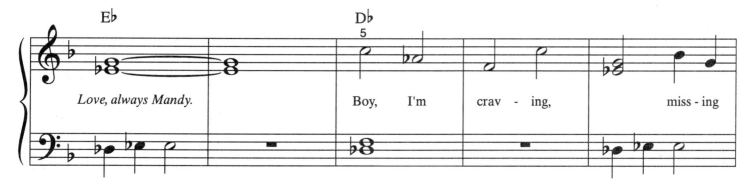

Love, always Mandy.   Boy, I'm crav - ing,   miss - ing

D.S. % al Fine

you like can - dy._   So, ba - by,

Candy - 6 - 6

COULD I HAVE THIS KISS FOREVER

Words and Music by
DIANE WARREN
Arranged by RICHARD BRADLEY

Moderately slow (♩ = 160)

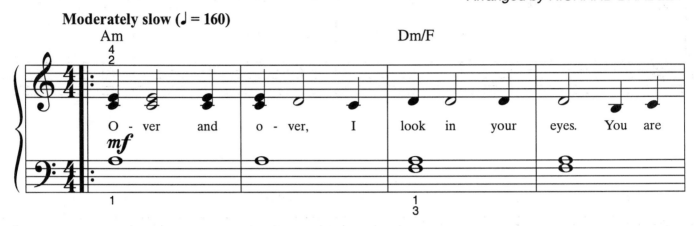

O- ver and o- ver, I look in your eyes. You are

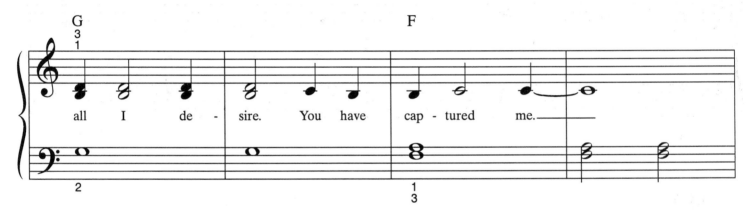

all I de- sire. You have cap- tured me.

I want to hold you, I want to be close to you.

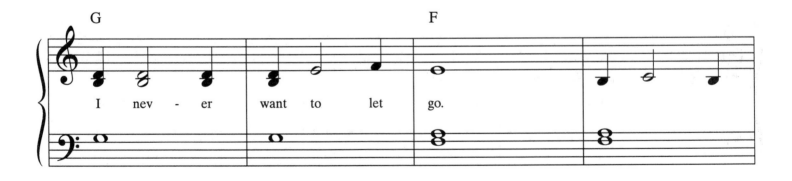

I nev- er want to let go.

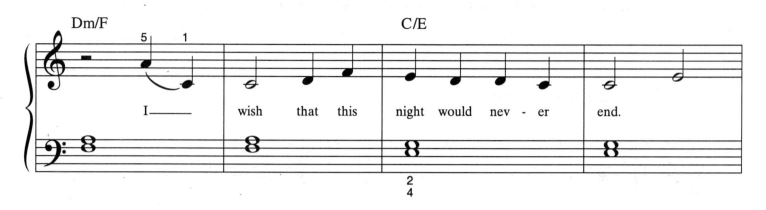

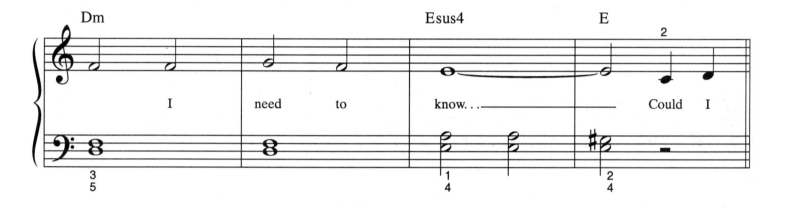

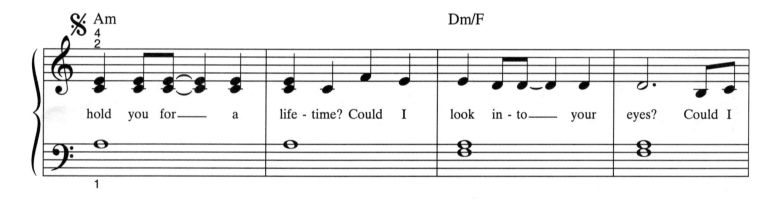

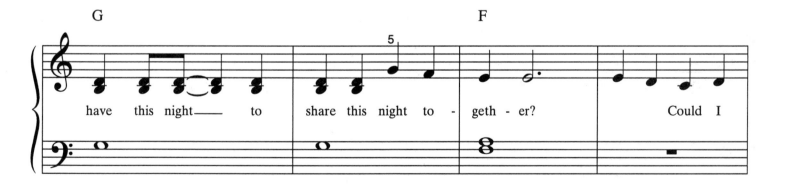

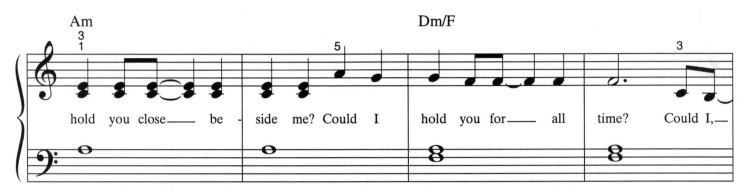

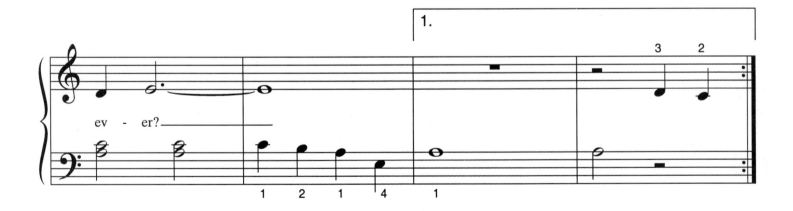

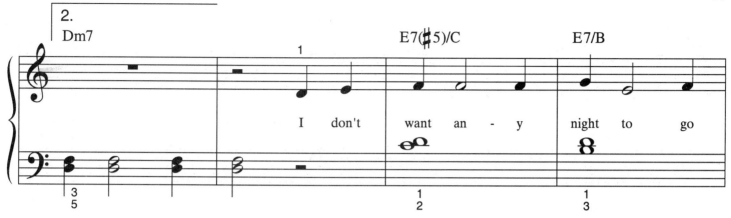

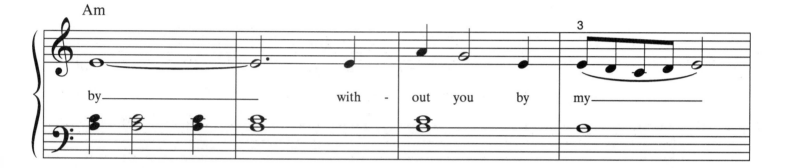

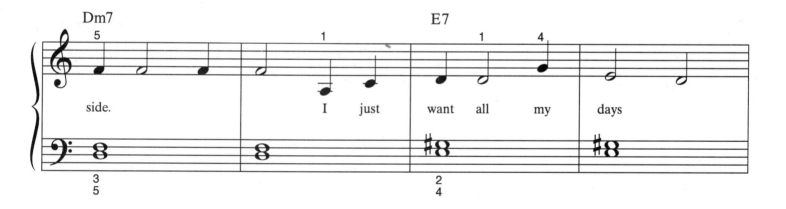

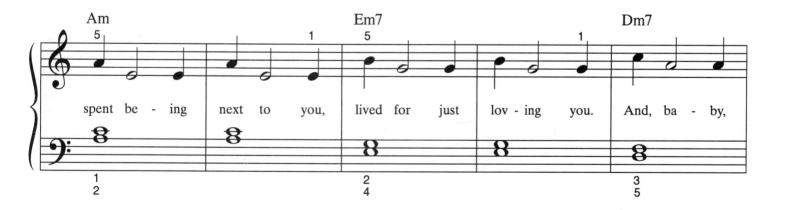

38

D.S. % al Coda

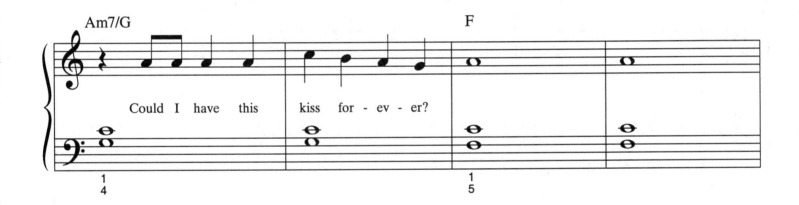

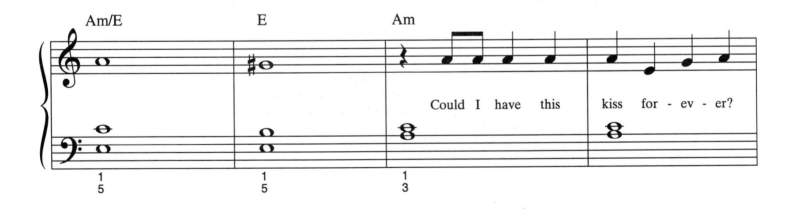

Could I Have This Kiss Forever - 6 - 5

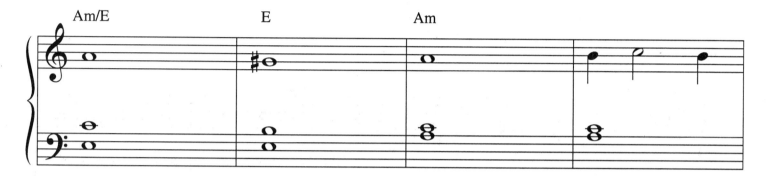

Verse 2:
Over and over, I've dreamed of this night.
Now you're here by my side, you are next to me.
I want to hold you, and touch you, and taste you,
And make you want no one but me.
I wish that this kiss could never end.
Oh, baby, please. . .

BREATHE

Words and Music by
STEPHANIE BENTLEY
and HOLLY LAMAR
Arranged by RICHARD BRADLEY

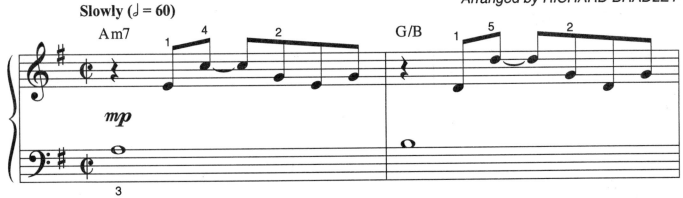

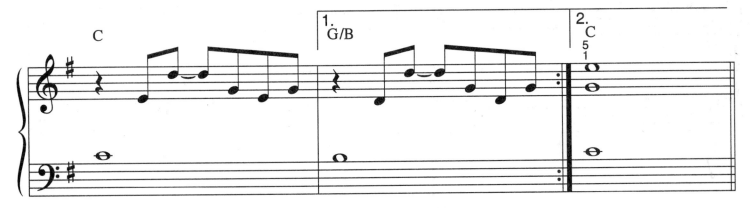

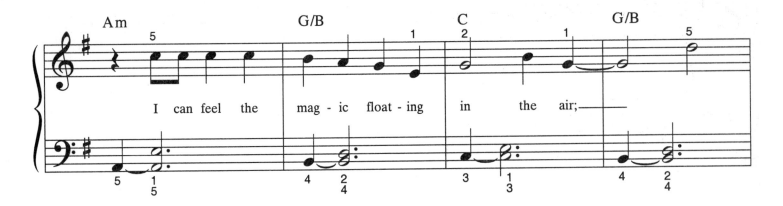

I can feel the mag - ic float - ing in the air;

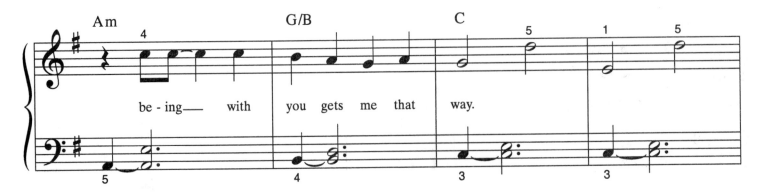

be - ing—— with you gets me that way.

Breathe - 5 - 1

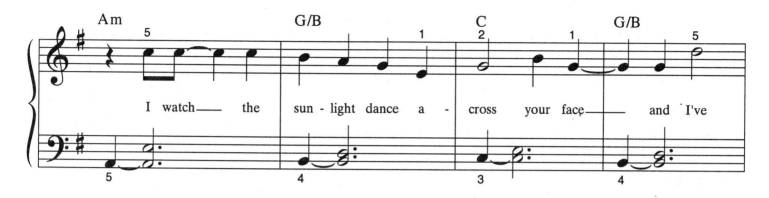

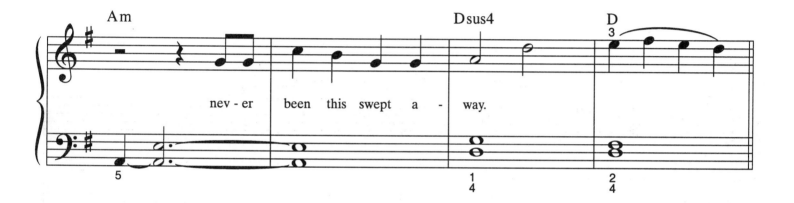

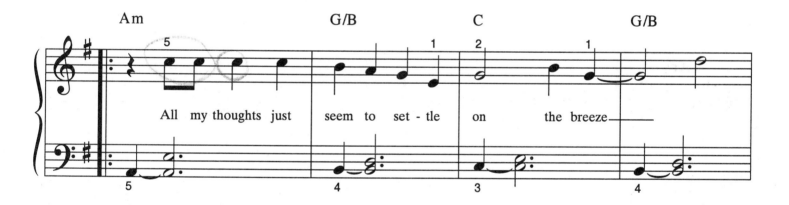

42

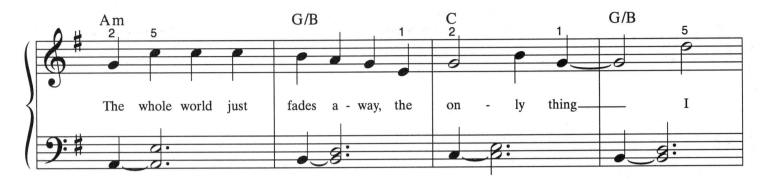

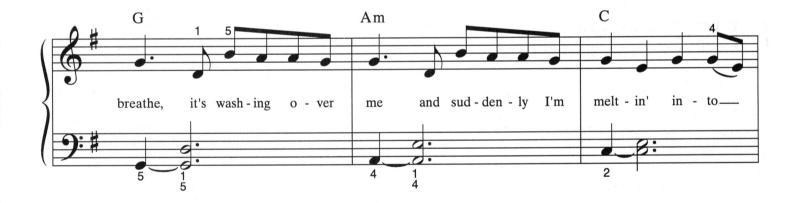

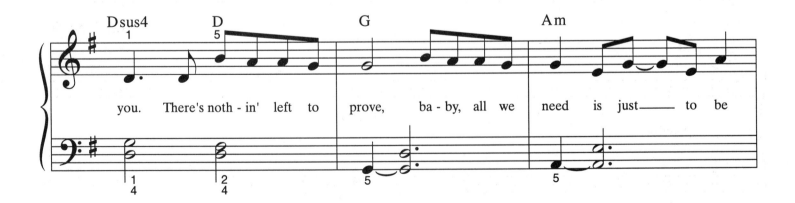

Breathe - 5 - 3

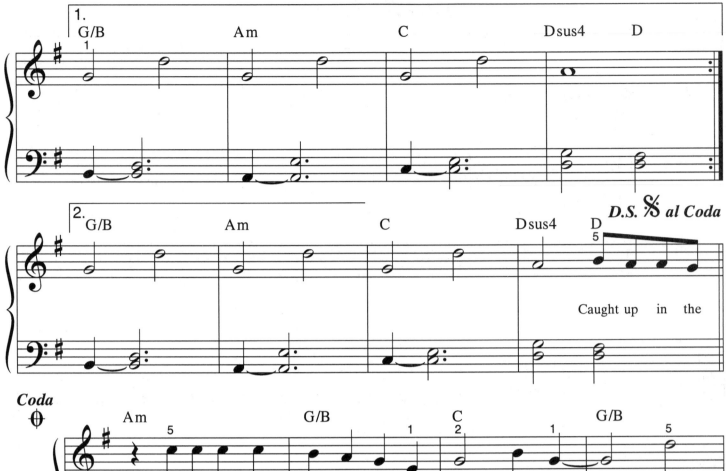

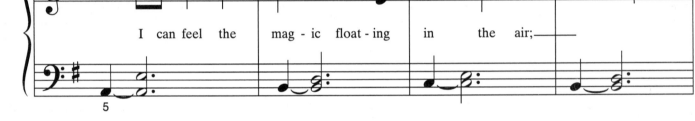

Caught up in the

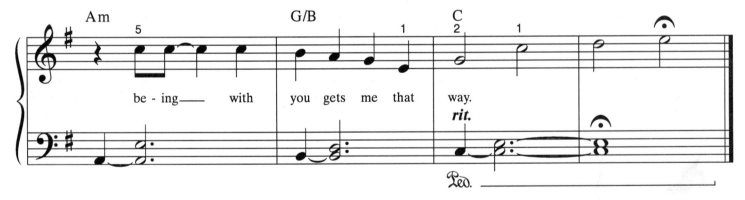

I can feel the mag - ic float - ing in the air;—

be - ing— with you gets me that way.

rit.

Additional Lyrics:
In a way, I know my heart is waking up
As all the walls come tumblin' down.
Closer than I've ever felt before
And I know and you know
There's no need for words right now.

FALLS APART

Words and Music by
SUGAR RAY and **DAVID KAHNE**
Arranged by RICHARD BRADLEY

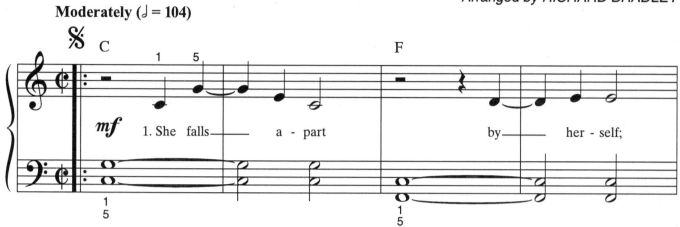

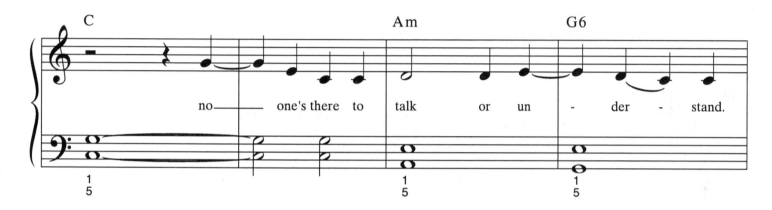

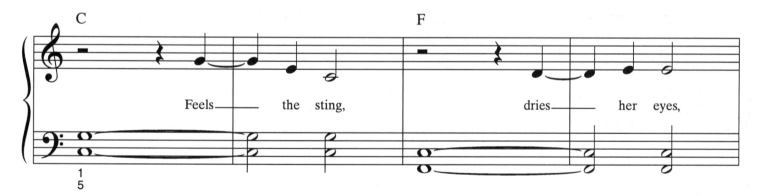

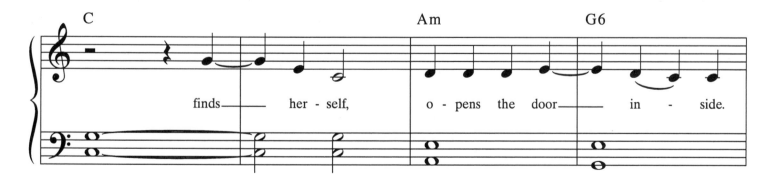

Falls Apart - 5 - 1

Play 1st and 2nd time only

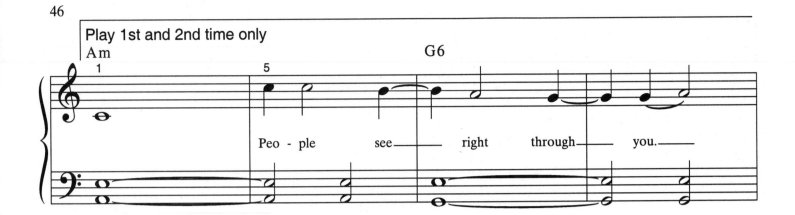

Peo - ple see right through you.

Ev - 'ry - one who knew you well

_ falls a - part, might as well,

day is long and noth - ing is wast - ed.

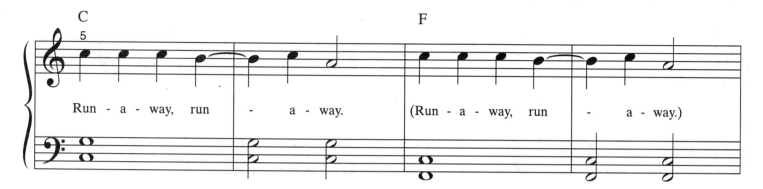

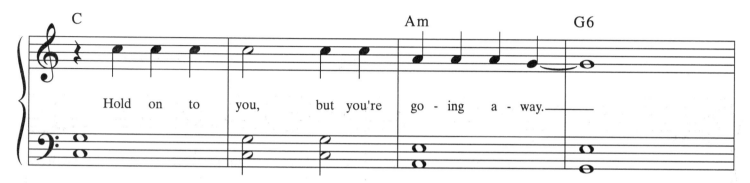

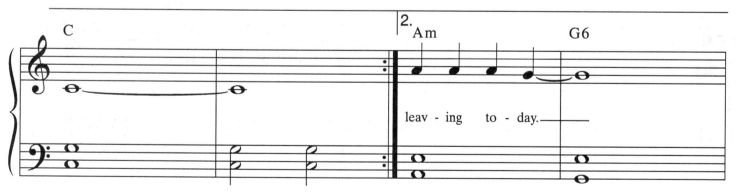

48

Some-times we feel a - round, it's get - ting———— I can't be down.

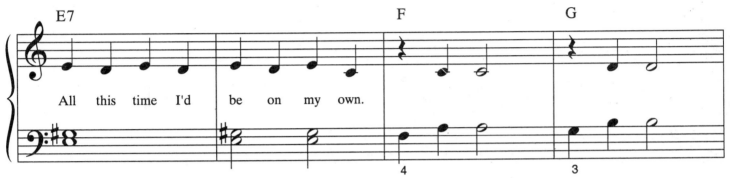

All this time I'd be on my own.

An - y thought of be - ing, yeah, it's time a - way, so I'm a - fraid I've

no - where to, no - where to, no - where to, no - where————

D.S. 𝄋 *al Coda* ⊕

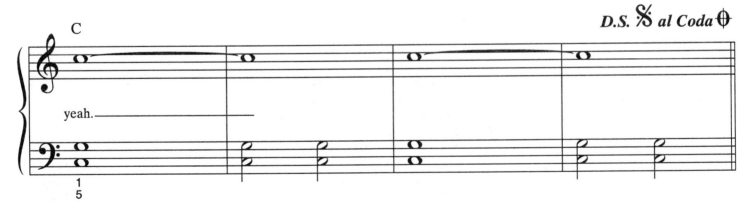

yeah.——————————

Coda

Hold you to - mor - row, but you're leav - ing to - day.

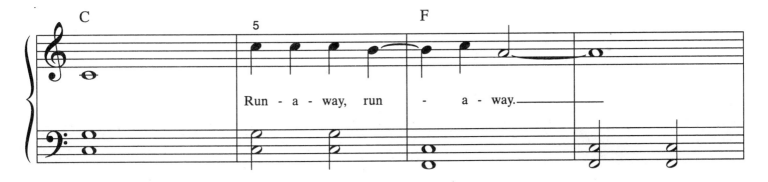

Run - a - way, run - a - way.

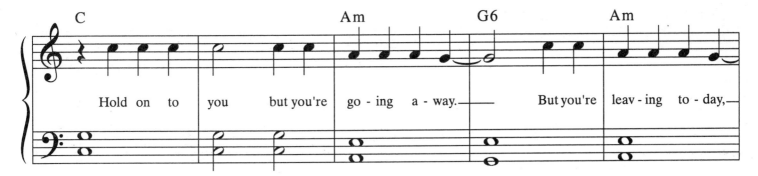

Hold on to you but you're go - ing a - way. But you're leav - ing to - day,

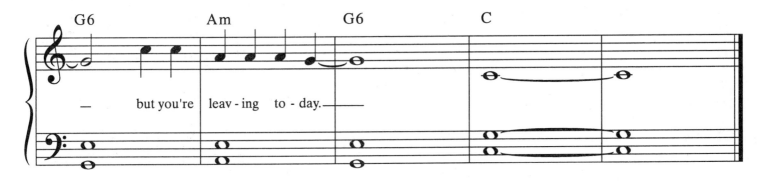

— but you're leav - ing to - day.

Verse 2:
You walk along by yourself.
There's no sound, nothing's changing.
They've gone away, left you there.
Emptiness, there's nothing you can share.
All those words that hurt you
More than you would let it show.
It comes apart by itself.
Always will and everything's wasted.
(To Chorus:)

Falls Apart - 5 - 5

FROM THE BOTTOM OF MY BROKEN HEART

Words and Music by
ERIC FOSTER WHITE
Arranged by RICHARD BRADLEY

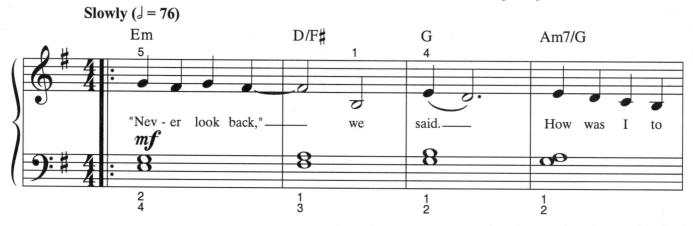

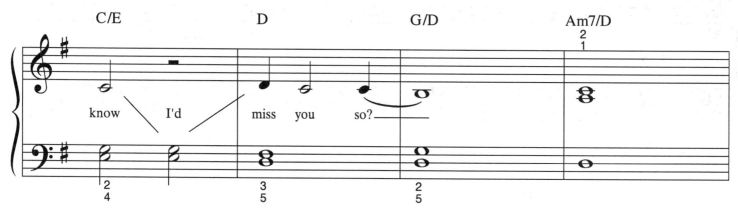

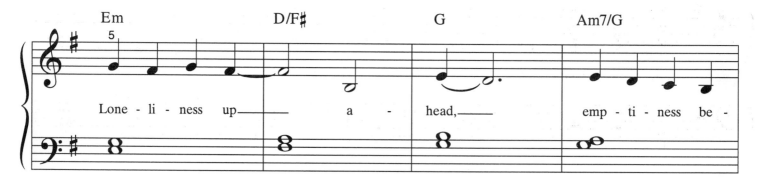

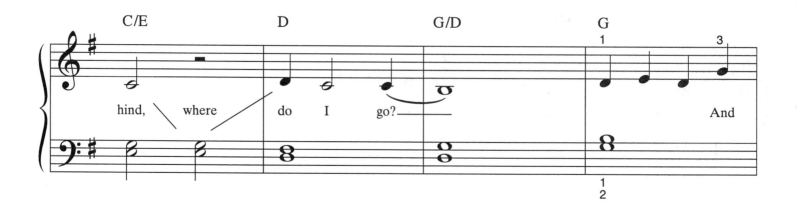

From the Bottom of My Broken Heart - 5 - 1

51

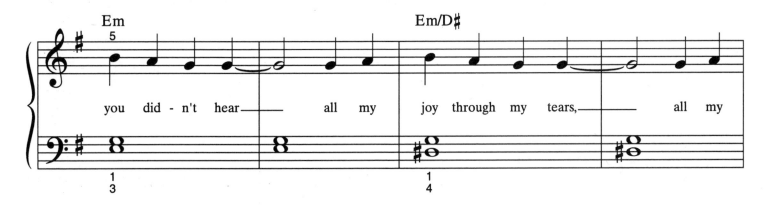

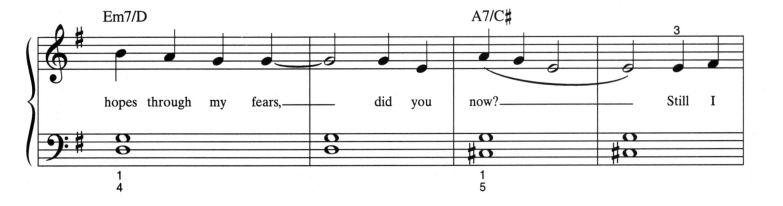

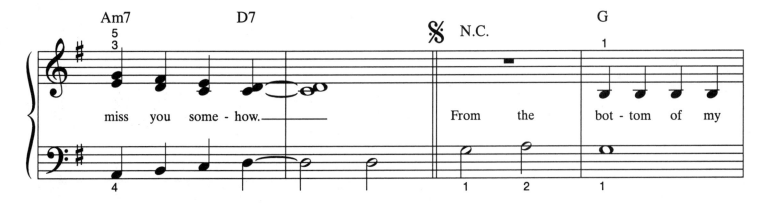

From the Bottom of My Broken Heart - 5 - 2

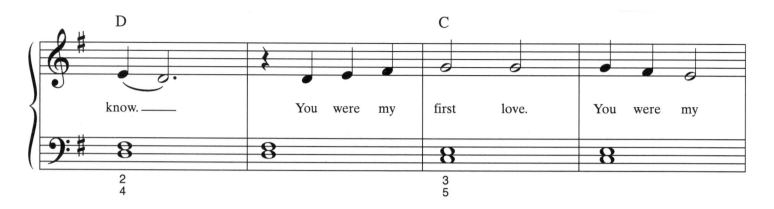

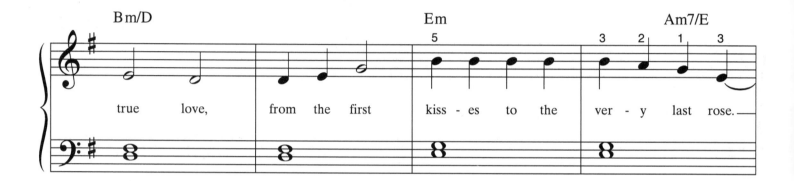

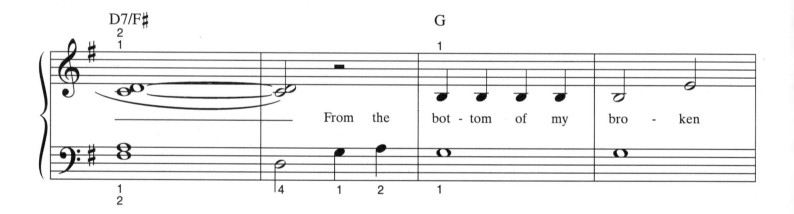

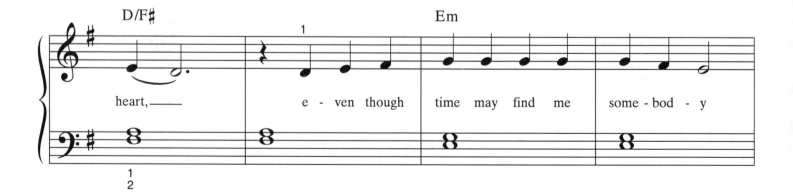

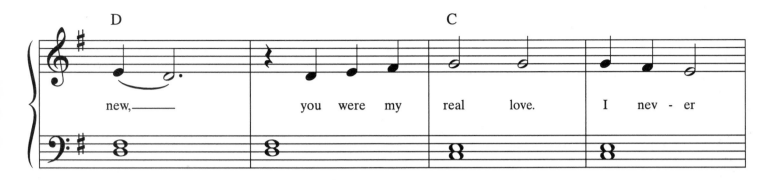

new,_____ you were my real love. I nev - er

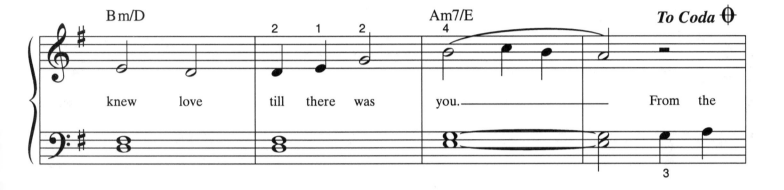

To Coda ⊕

knew love till there was you._____ From the

1.

bot - tom of my bro - ken_____ heart._____

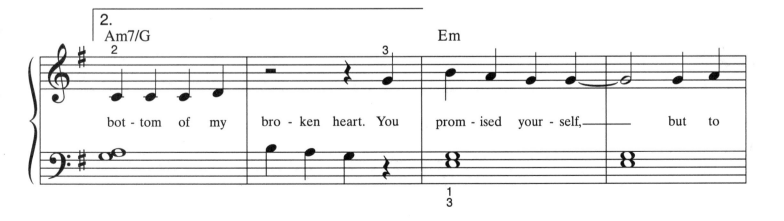

2.

bot - tom of my bro - ken heart. You prom - ised your - self,_____ but to

54

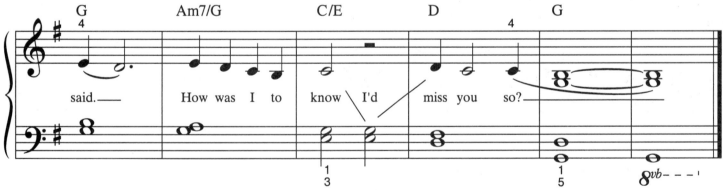

Verse 2:
"Baby," I said, "please stay.
Give our love a chance for one more day."
We could have worked things out.
Taking time is what love's all about.
But you put a dart through my dreams,
Through my heart,
And I'm back where I started again.
Never thought it would end.

I LEARNED FROM THE BEST

Words and Music by
DIANE WARREN
Arranged by RICHARD BRADLEY

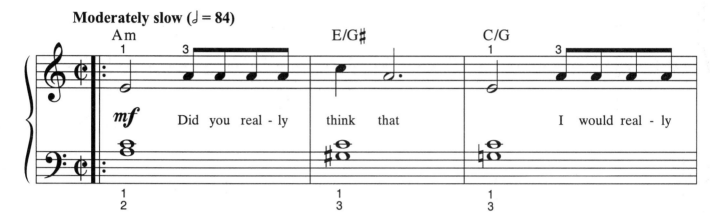

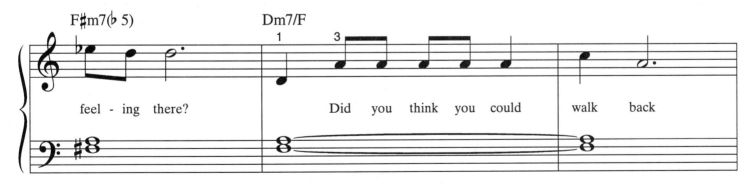

I Learned From the Best - 5 - 1

56

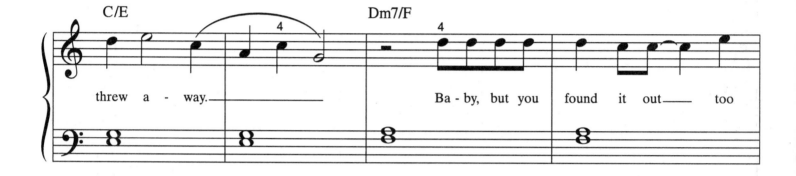

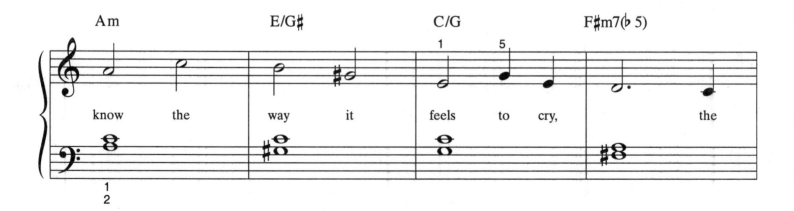

I Learned From the Best - 5 - 2

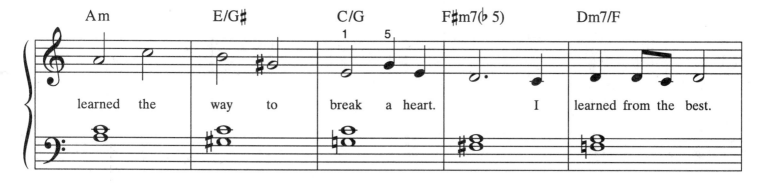

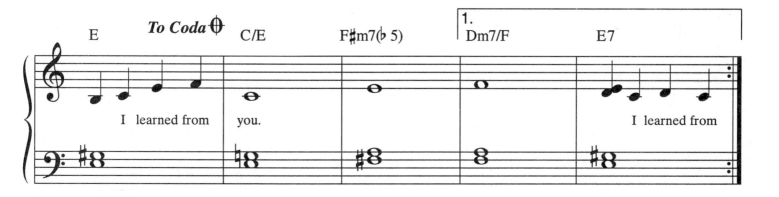

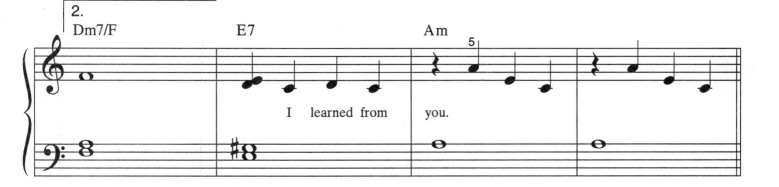

So, when all you've got are sleep - less nights,

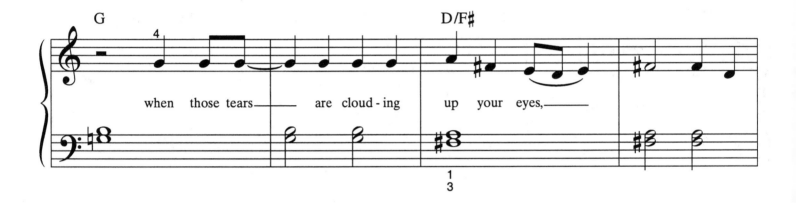

when those tears are cloud - ing up your eyes,

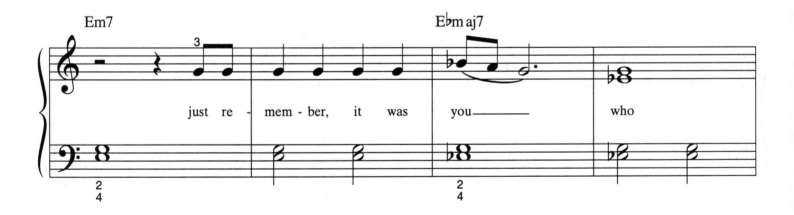

just re - mem - ber, it was you who

D.S. 𝄉 *al Coda* 𝄌

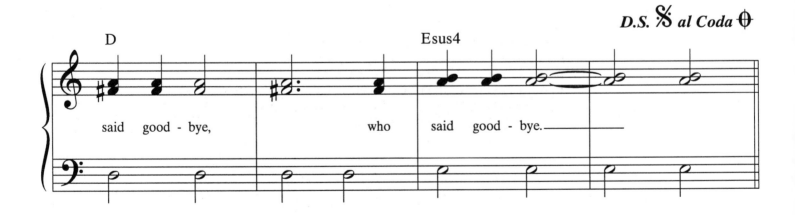

said good - bye, who said good - bye.

Coda

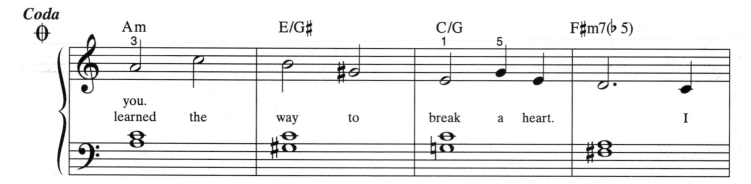

Am   E/G♯   C/G   F♯m7(♭5)

you.
learned   the   way   to   break   a   heart.   I

Dm7/F   E7   C/E   F♯m7(♭5)

learned from the best.   I   learned from   you.   I

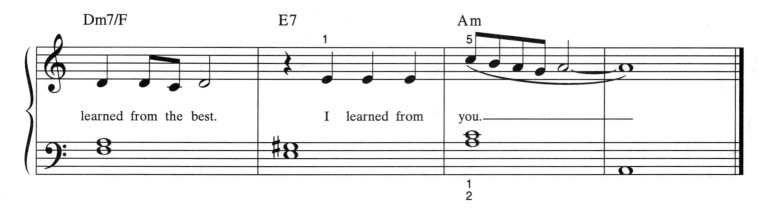

Dm7/F   E7   Am

learned from the best.   I   learned from   you._____

Verse 2:
I remember cold nights, tears that would never dry.
How you shattered my world with your good-bye.
Would've sold my soul then, just to have you back again.
Now you are the last thing on my mind.
Now you say you're sorry and you've changed your ways.
Sorry, but you changed your ways too late.

GRADUATION
(FRIENDS FOREVER)

Words and Music by
COLLEEN FITZPATRICK
and JOSH DEUTSCH
Arranged by RICHARD BRADLEY

Slow shuffle (♩ = 80)

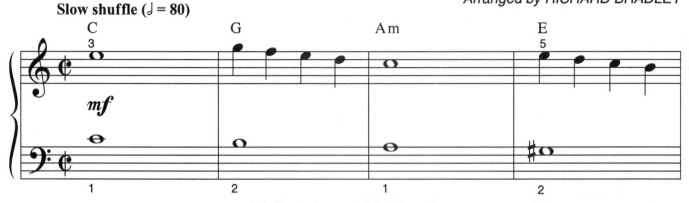

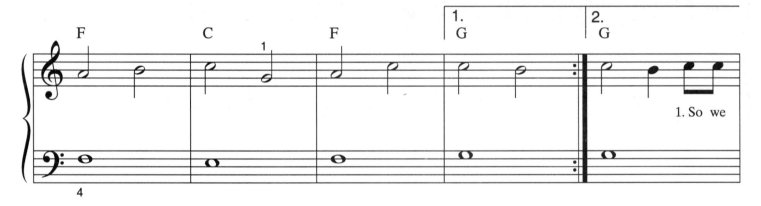

Graduation - 6 - 1

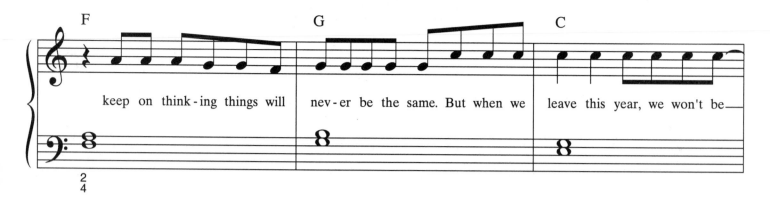

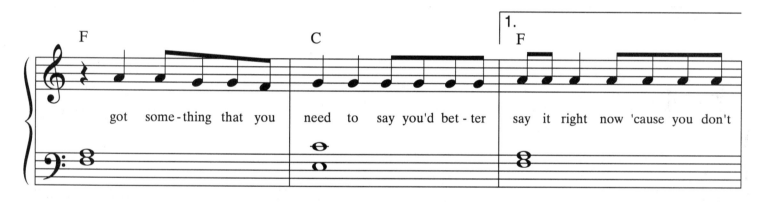

life's   not   fair.   *And this is how it feels.*

Chorus:

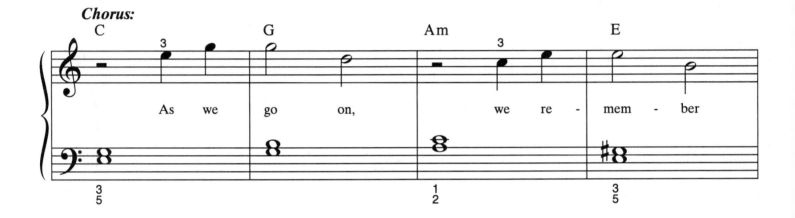

As   we   go   on,   we re - mem - ber

all   the   times   we   had   to - geth - er.

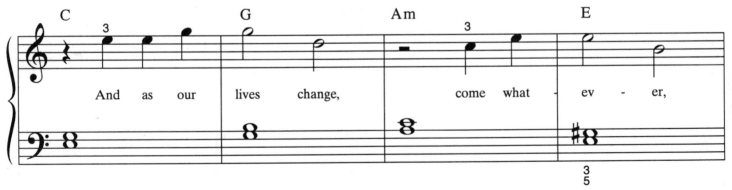

And   as   our   lives   change,   come   what - ev - er,

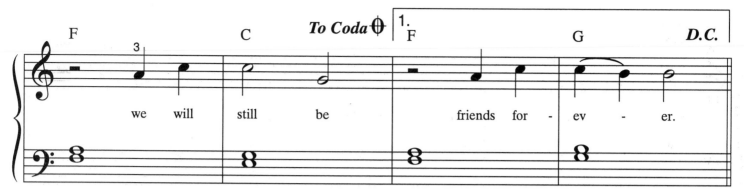

we will still be friends for - ev - er.

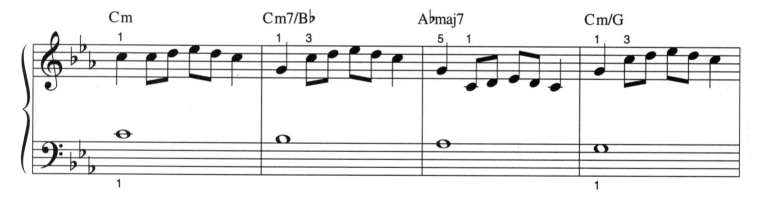

2. friends for - ev - er.

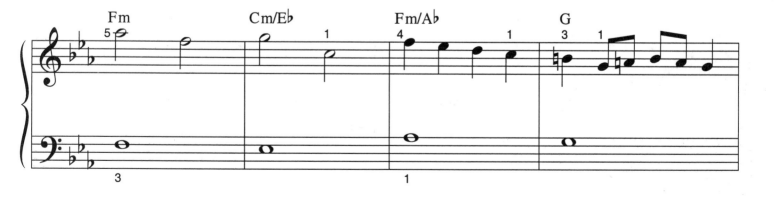

Graduation - 6 - 4

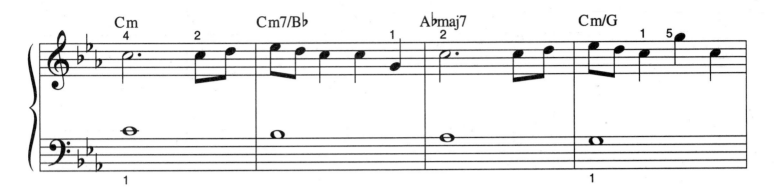

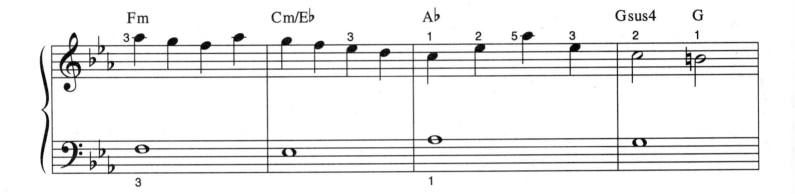

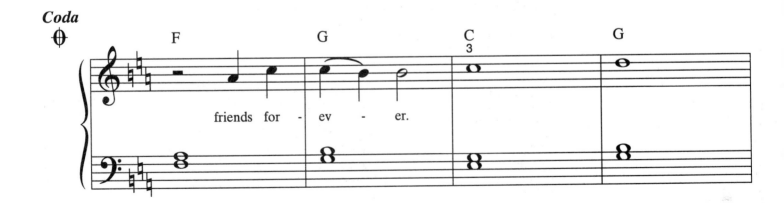

friends for - ev - er.

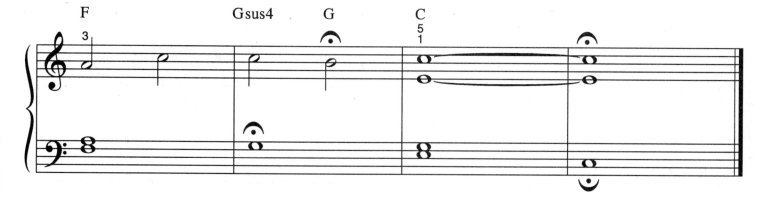

Verse 2:

'Cause we're moving on and we can't slow down.
These memories are playing like film without sound
And I keep thinking of that night in June.
I didn't know much of love but it came too soon.
And there was me and you and when we got real blue,
We'd stay at home talking on the telephone,
And we would get so excited and we'd get so scared,
Laughing at ourselves, thinking life's not fair.

Verse 3:

So if we get big jobs and we make big money,
When we look back at now, will our jokes still be funny?
Will we still remember everything we learned in school,
Still be trying to break every single rule?
Will little brainy Bobby be the stockbroker man?
Can Heather find a job that won't interfere with her tan?
I keep, keep thinking that it's not goodbye,
Keep on thinking it's our time to fly.
And this is how it feels . . .

Verse 4:

Will we think about tomorrow like we think about now?
Can we survive it out there, can we make it somehow?
I guess I thought that this would never end,
And suddenly it's like we're women and men.
Will the past be a shadow that will follow us around?
Will the memories fade when I leave this town?
I keep, keep thinking that it's not goodbye,
Keep thinking it's our time to fly.

I TURN TO YOU

Words and Music by
DIANE WARREN
Arranged by RICHARD BRADLEY

Slowly (♩ = 76)

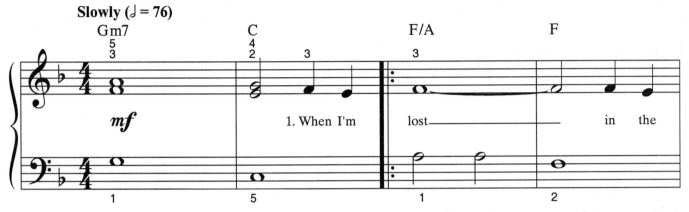

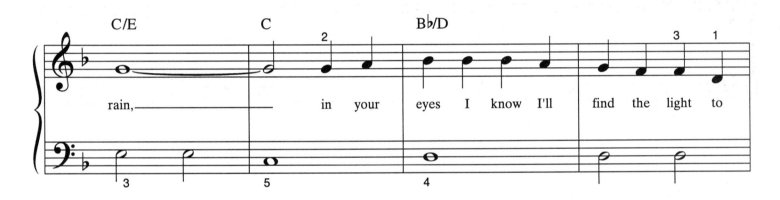

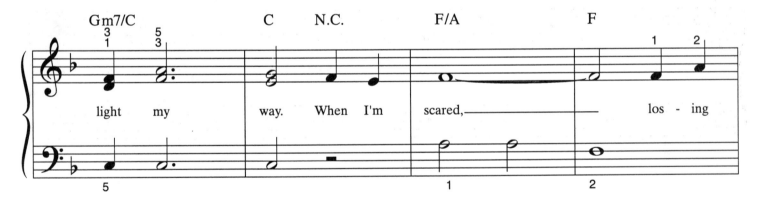

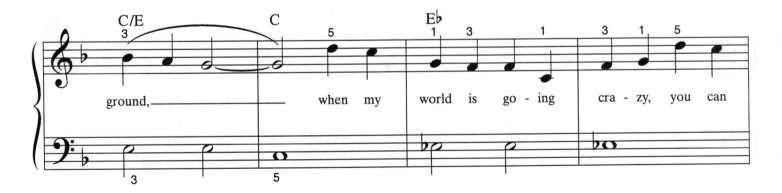

I Turn to You - 6 - 1

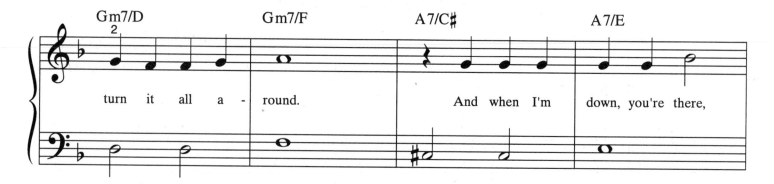

Gm7/D — Gm7/F — A7/C♯ — A7/E

turn it all a - round. And when I'm down, you're there,

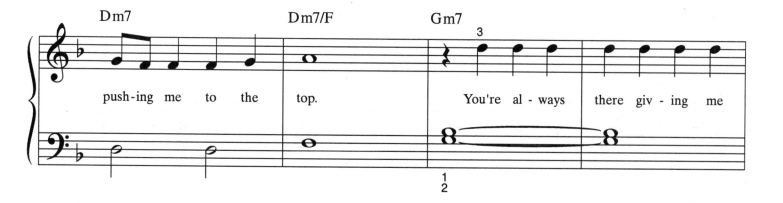

Dm7 — Dm7/F — Gm7

push-ing me to the top. You're al - ways there giv - ing me

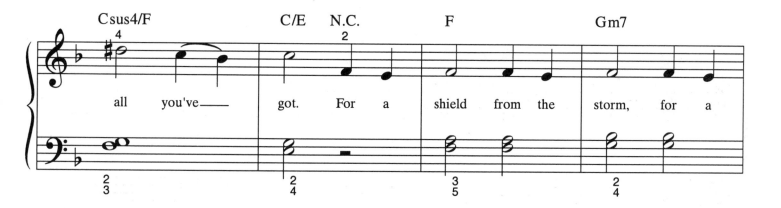

Csus4/F — C/E N.C. — F — Gm7

all you've_____ got. For a shield from the storm, for a

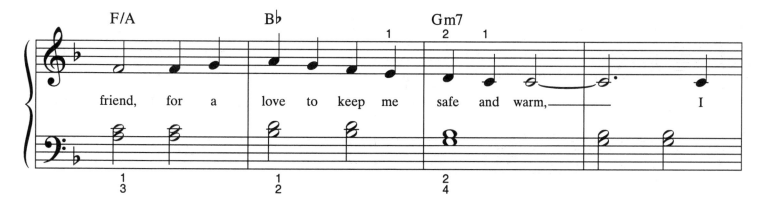

F/A — B♭ — Gm7

friend, for a love to keep me safe and warm,_____ I

68

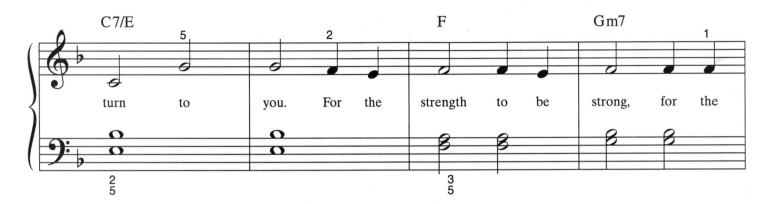

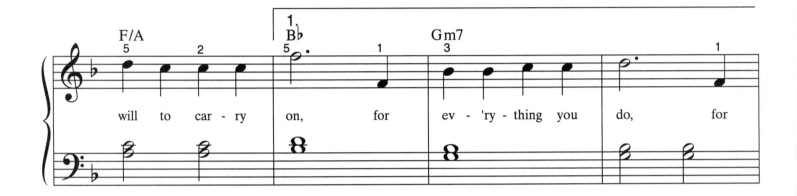

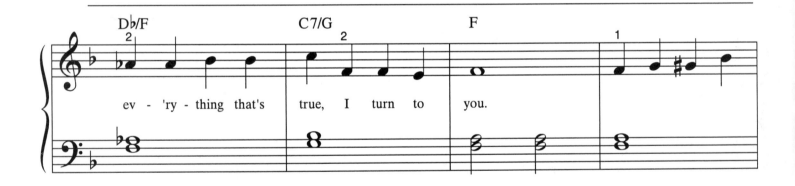

ev - 'ry - thing you do, I turn to you.

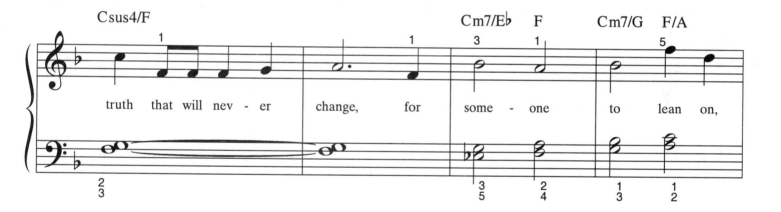

For the arms to be my shel - ter through all the rain, for

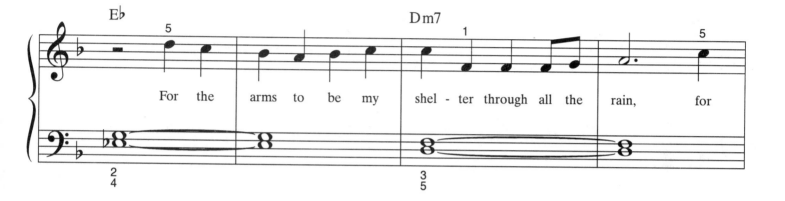

truth that will nev - er change, for some - one to lean on,

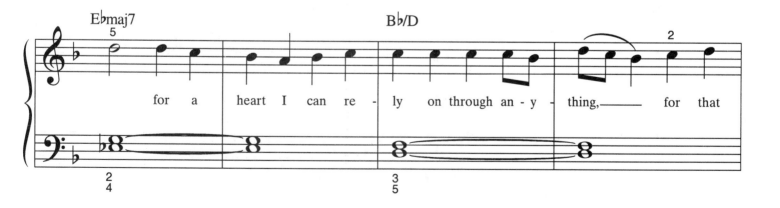

for a heart I can re - ly on through an - y - thing, for that

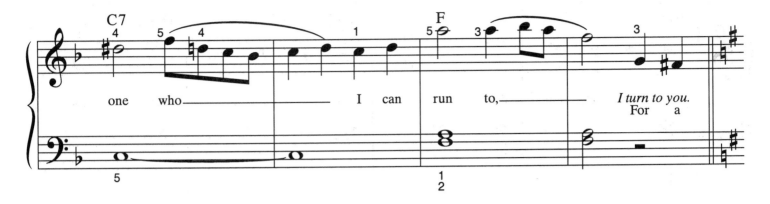

one who_____ I can run to,_____ *I turn to you.*
For a

shield from the storm, for a friend, for a love to keep me

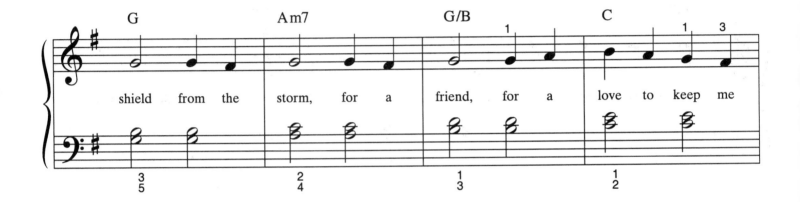

safe and warm,_____ I turn to you. For the

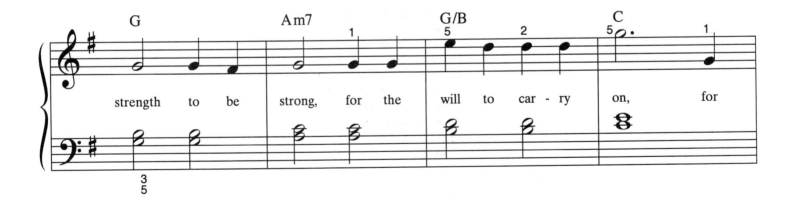

strength to be strong, for the will to car-ry on, for

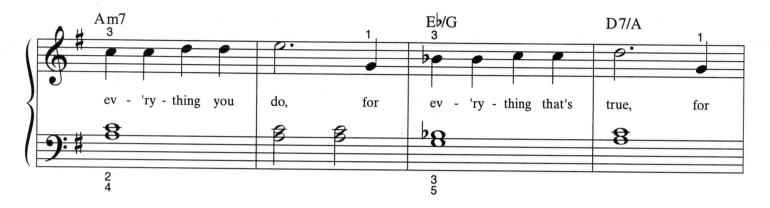

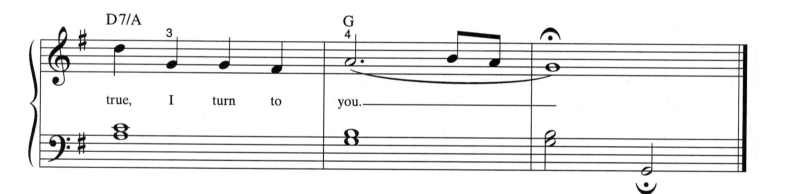

Verse 2:
When I lose the will to win,
I just reach for you
And I can reach the sky again.
I can do anything
'Cause your love is so amazing,
'Cause your love inspires me.
And when I need a friend,
You're always on my side,
Giving me faith,
Taking me through the night.

I WANT YOU TO NEED ME

Words and Music by
DIANE WARREN
Arranged by RICHARD BRADLEY

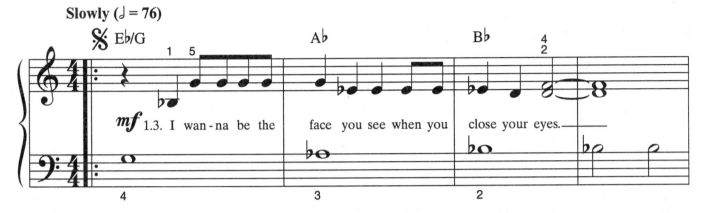

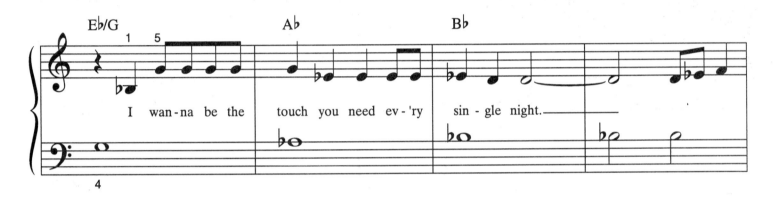

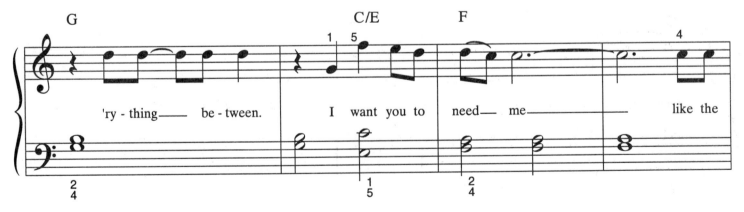

I Want You to Need Me - 5 - 1

I Want You to Need Me - 5 - 2

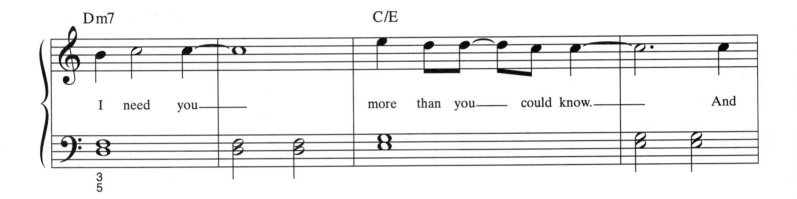

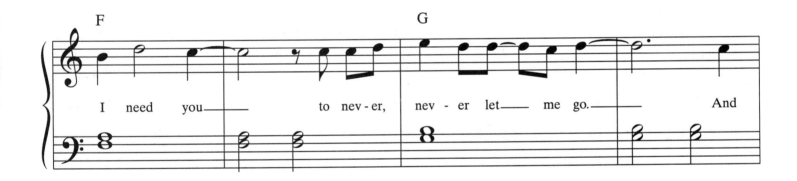

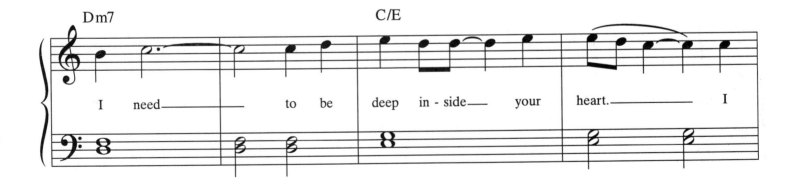

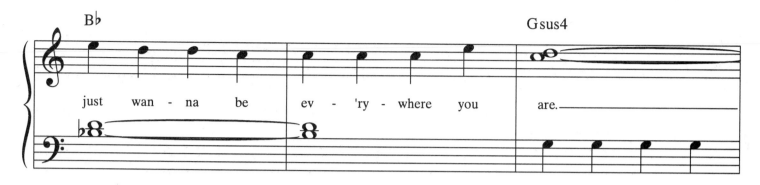

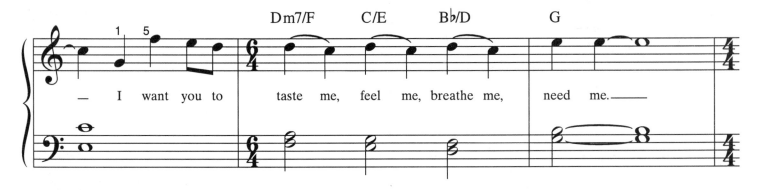

Verse 2:
I wanna be the eyes
That look deep into your soul.
I wanna be the world to you.
I just want it all.
I wanna be your deepest kiss,
The answer to your every wish,
And all you ever need.

I WAS BORN TO LOVE YOU

Words and Music by
ERIC CARMEN and ANDY GOLDMARK
Arranged by RICHARD BRADLEY

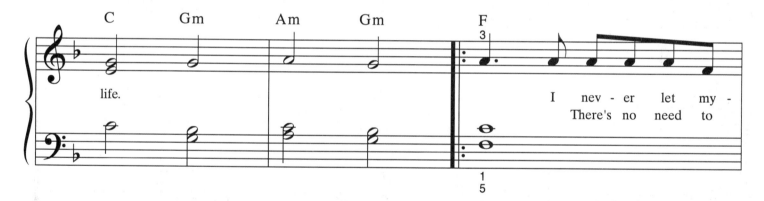

I Was Born to Love You - 3 - 1

78

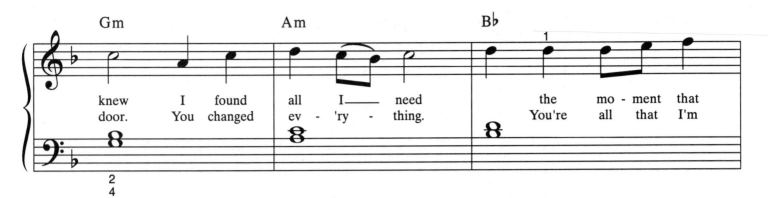

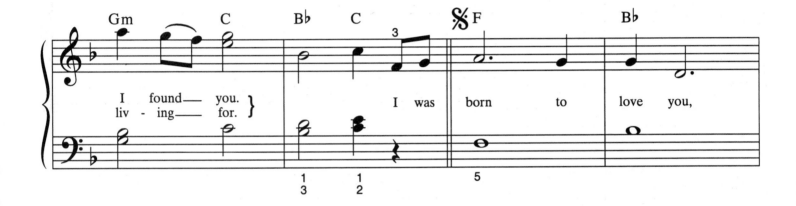

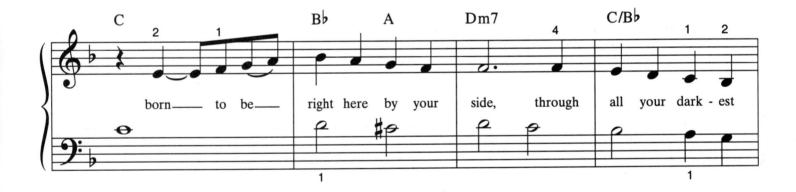

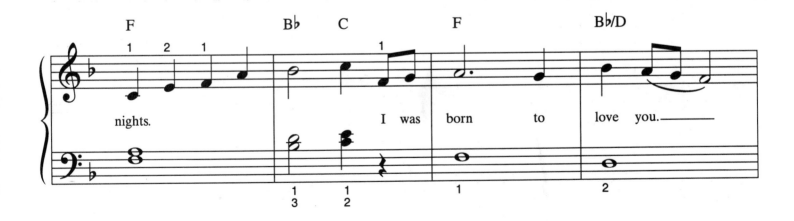

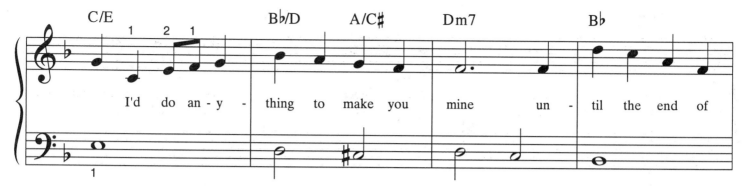

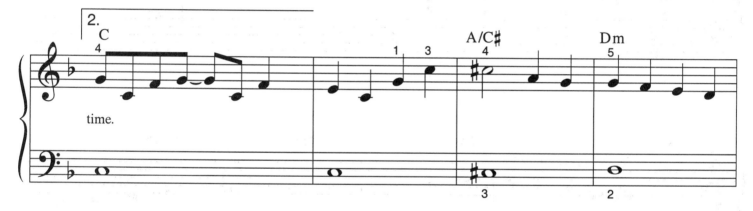

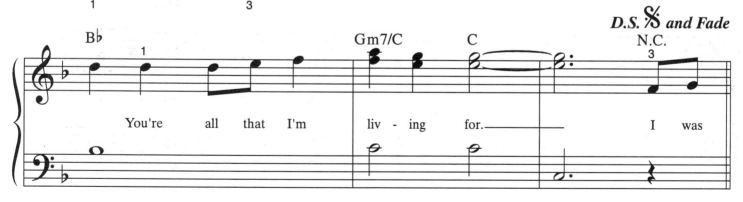

I Was Born to Love You - 3 - 3

IF I DIDN'T LOVE YOU

Words and Music by
JUNIOR MILES and
BRUCE ROBERTS
Arranged by RICHARD BRADLEY

Slowly (♩ = 72)

1. If I did-n;t love you,_____ I'd be safe from harm._____

_ I would nev-er find my-self_____ lost in-side your arms.

If I did-n't love you, I'd nev-er feel the pain_____

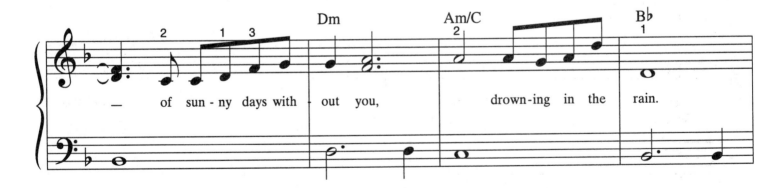

_ of sun-ny days with-out you, drown-ing in the rain.

If I Didn't Love You - 6 - 1

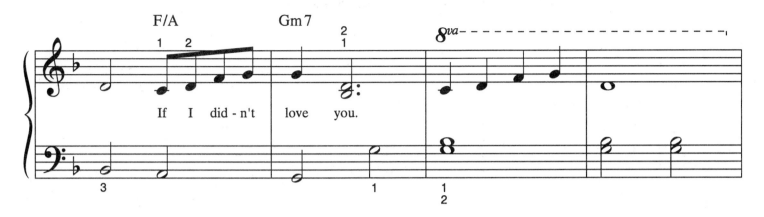

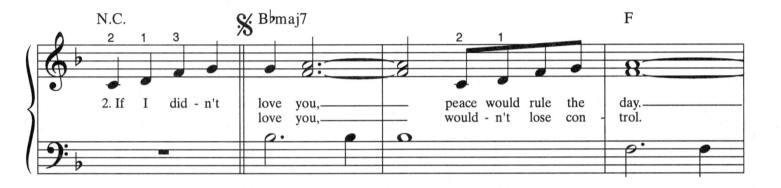

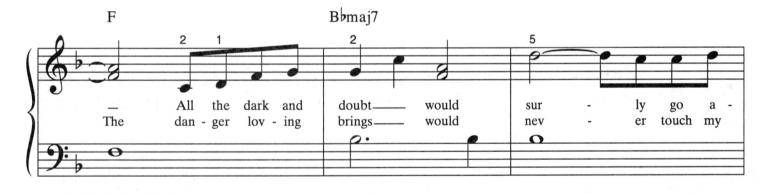

82

F/C

cost_____ of liv - ing ev - 'ry end - less day if our love is
die_____ if you should ev - er say to me, "I'm sor - ry, good -

Dm7 Am/C

Bb *To Coda* ⊕   F/A   Gm

lost.
bye."   If I did-n't love you.

8va

N.C.   F

If I did-n't love you._____   And yet you make

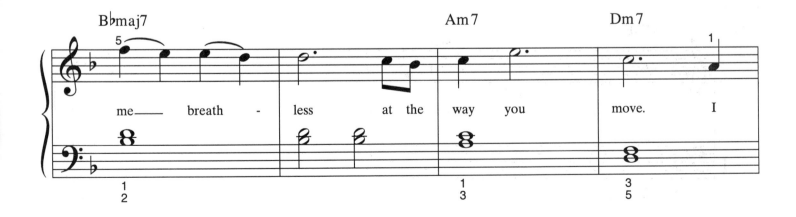

Bbmaj7   Am7   Dm7

me____ breath - less   at the way you   move.   I

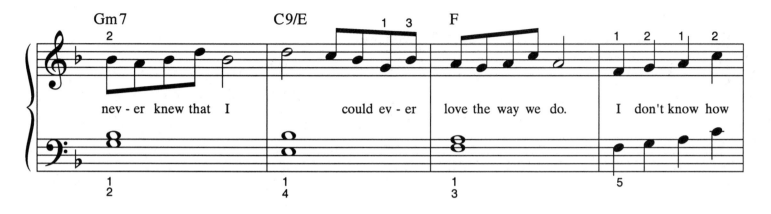

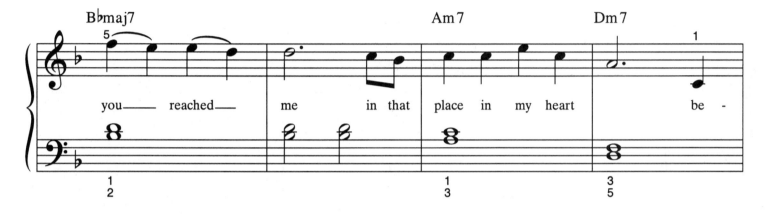

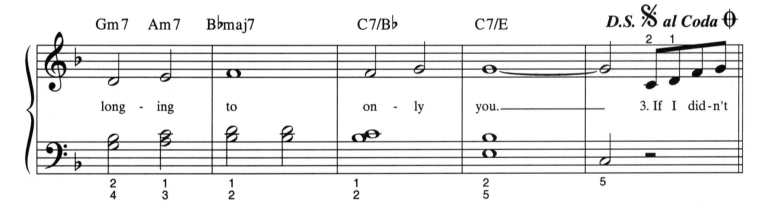

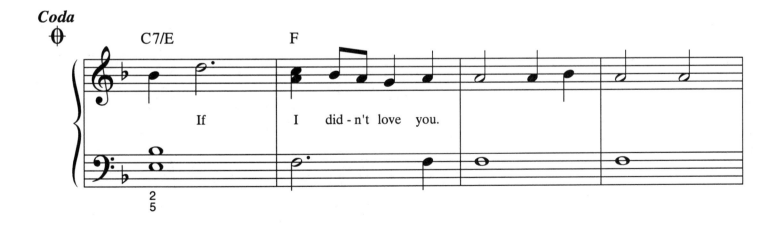

84

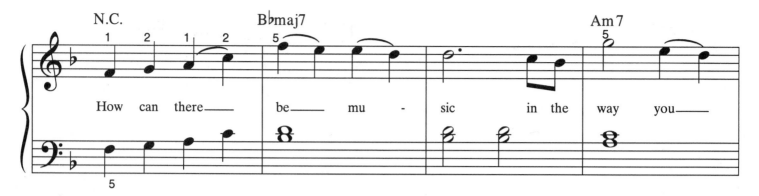

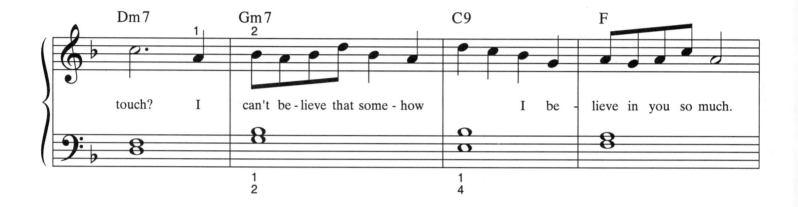

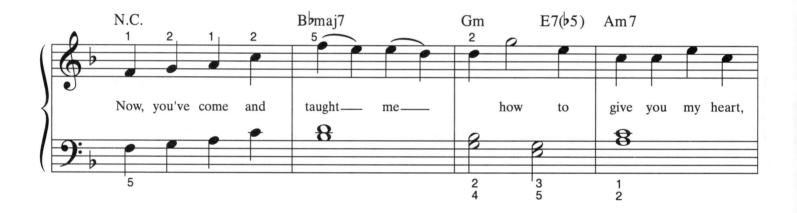

If I Didn't Love You - 6 - 5

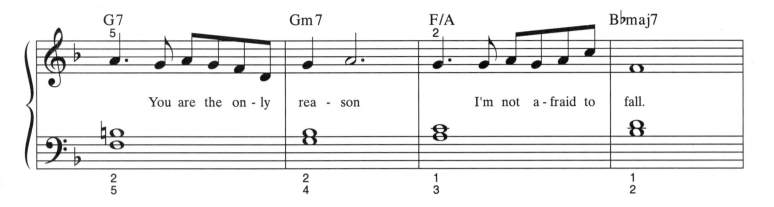

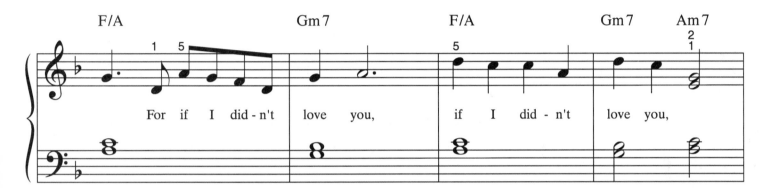

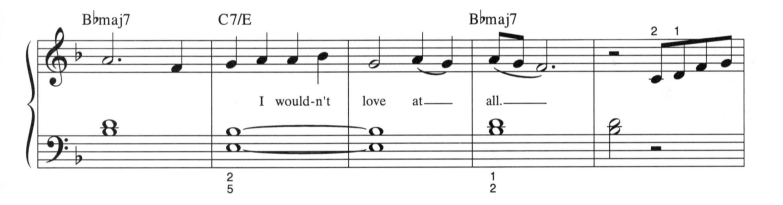

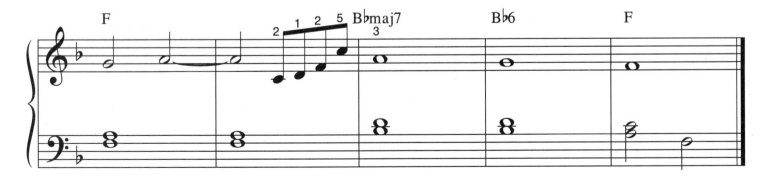

If I Didn't Love You - 6 - 6

IT'S GONNA BE ME

Words and Music by
MAX MARTIN, RAMI
and ANDREAS CARLSSON
Arranged by RICHARD BRADLEY

Moderately slow (♩ = 82)

1. You might've been hurt, babe,

that ain't no lie. You've seen them all come and go,

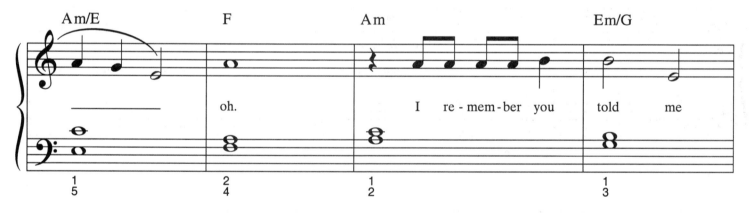

oh. I re-mem-ber you told me

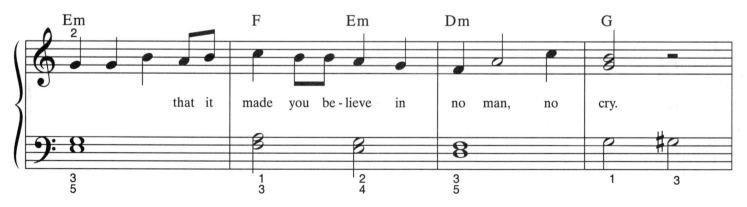

that it made you be-lieve in no man, no cry.

It's Gonna Be Me - 6 - 1

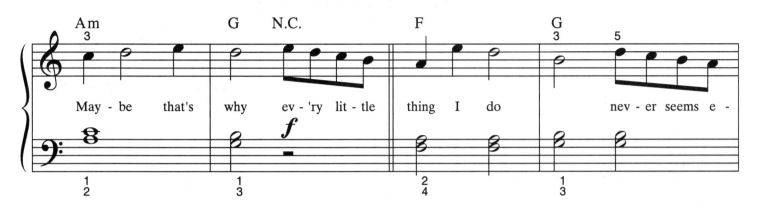

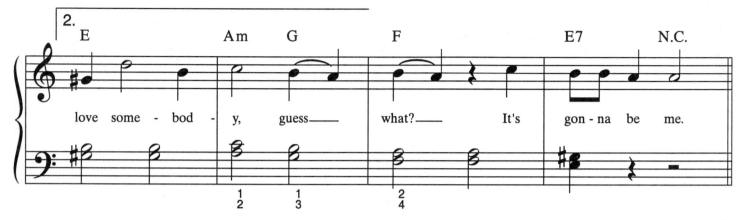

love some - bod - y, guess_____ what?_____ It's gon - na be me.

(It's gonna be me.) *Ooh, yeah, yeah.*

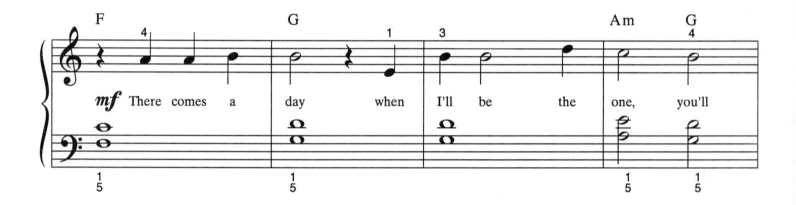

mf There comes a day when I'll be the one, you'll

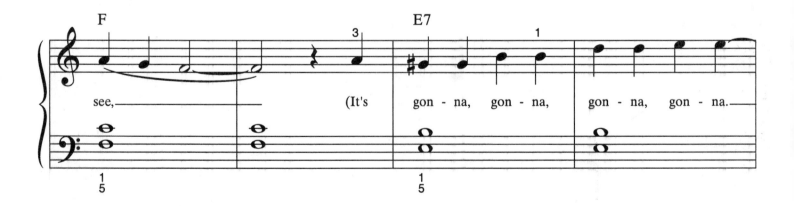

see,_____ (It's gon - na, gon - na, gon - na, gon - na._____

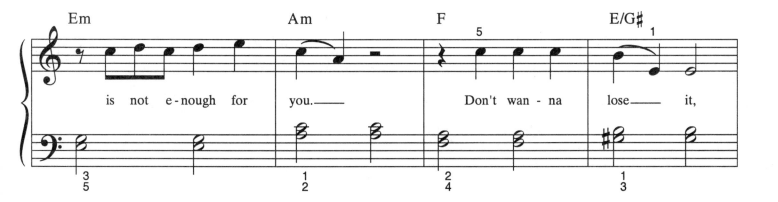

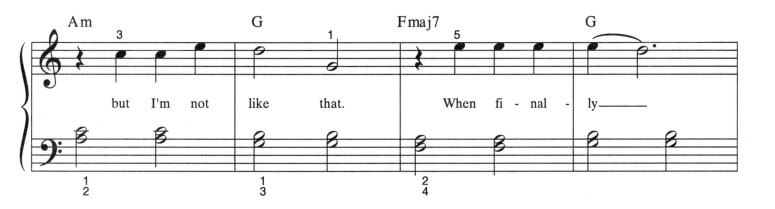

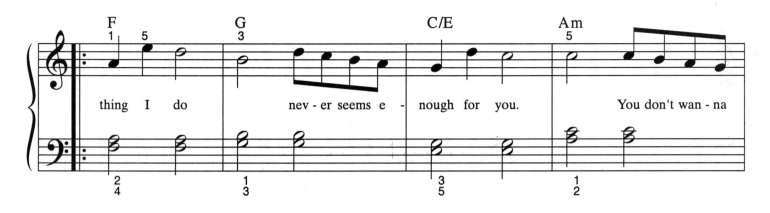

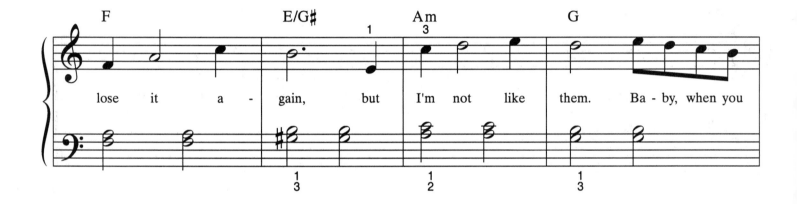

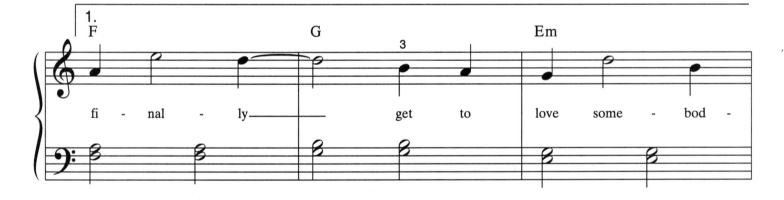

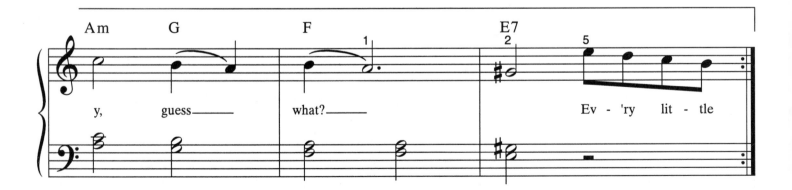

Verse 2:
You've got no choice, babe,
But to move on, you know
There ain't no time to waste,
'Cause you're just too blind to see.
But in the end you know it's gonna be me.
You can't deny,
So just tell me why...
(To Chorus:)

MARIA MARIA

Words and Music by
**WYCLEF JEAN, JERRY DUPLESSIS,
CARLOS SANTANA, KARL PERAZZO and RAUL REKOW**
Arranged by RICHARD BRADLEY

Moderately (♩ = 98)

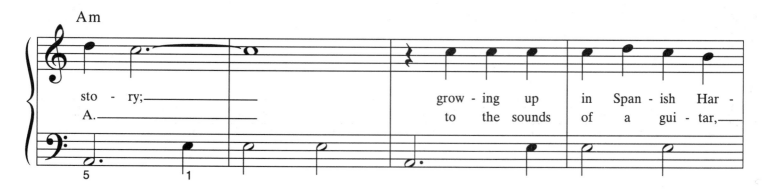

Maria Maria - 4 - 1

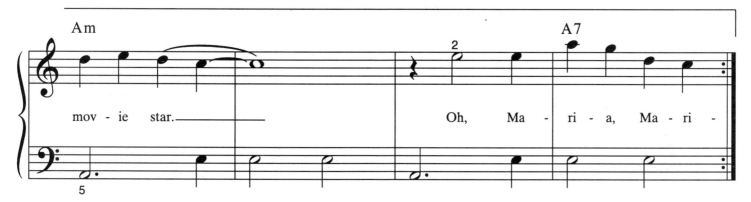

Am ... A7

mov - ie star._____ Oh, Ma - ri - a, Ma - ri -

2. 4.
E/B ... Am

played by Car - los San - ta - na.

To Coda

N.C. Am

Stop the loot-ing, stop the shoot-ing, pick -

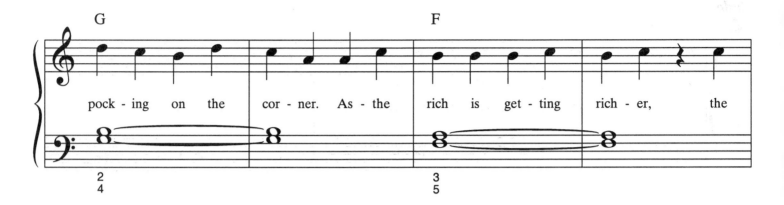

G   F

pock - ing on the   cor - ner. As - the   rich is get - ting   rich - er,   the

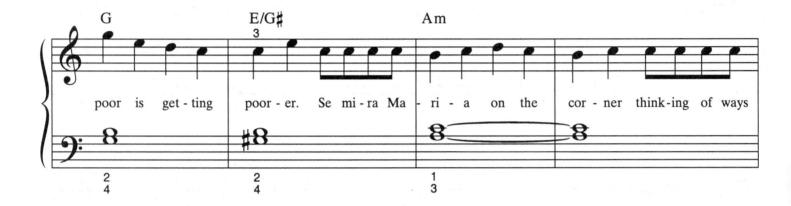

G   E/G♯   Am

poor is get - ting   poor - er. Se mi - ra Ma   ri - a on the   cor - ner think-ing of ways

G   F

to make it bet -   ter. In my   mail - box there's an e - vic -   tion ——— let - ter.

G   E/G♯   Am   **D.S. 𝄋 al Coda** ⊕

Some - bod - y just —— said,   "See you —— lat - er."   Yeah. —— Ma - ri - a, Ma - ri -

Coda

Ma - ri - a, you know you're my lov - er.

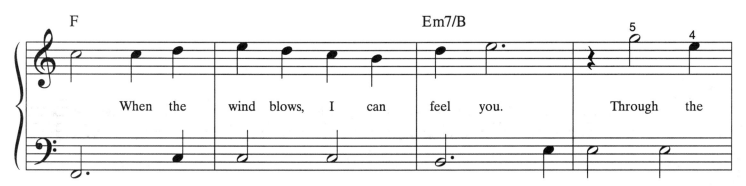

When the wind blows, I can feel you. Through the

weath - er and e - ven when we are a - part,

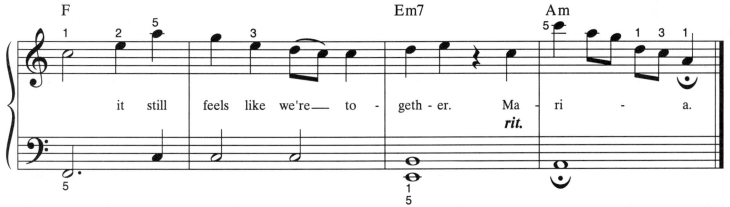

it still feels like we're to - geth - er. Ma - ri - a.

rit.

Verse 2:
I said, "A la favella los colores."
The streets are getting hotter.
There is no water
To put out the fire.
Mi canto, la esperanza.
Se mira Maria on the corner
Thinking of ways to make it better.
Then I looked up in the sky
Hoping the days of paradise.

THE ONE

Words and Music by
MAX MARTIN and BRIAN T. LITTRELL
Arranged by RICHARD BRADLEY

Moderately (♩ = 112)

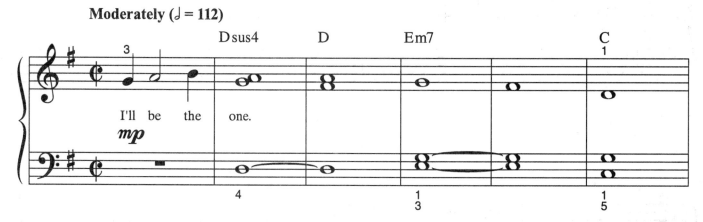

I'll be the one.

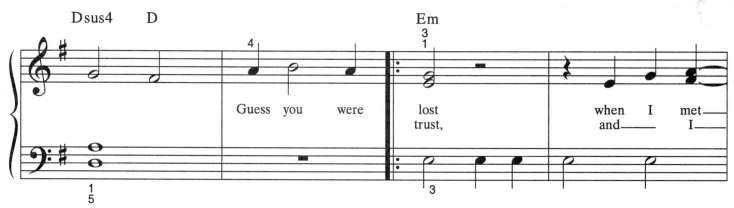

Guess you were / lost trust, / when I met— / and— I

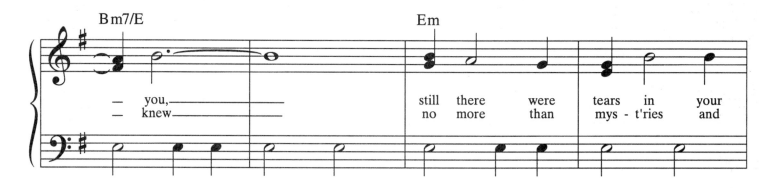

— you, / — knew— / still no there more were than / tears mys - in t'ries your and

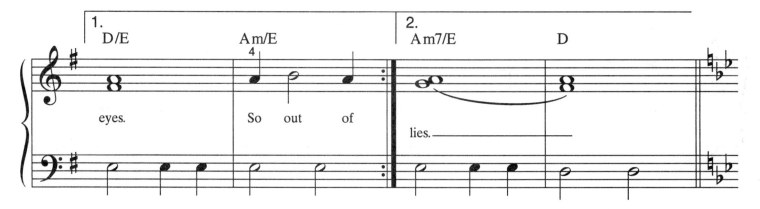

eyes. / So out of / lies.—

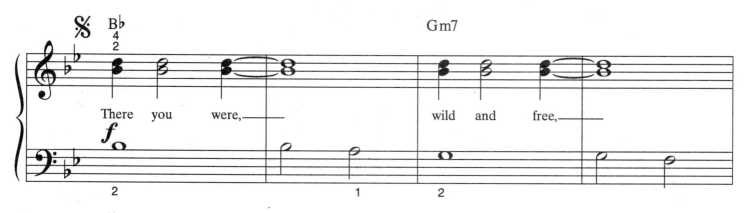

There you were,——— wild and free,———

reach - ing out——— like you need - ed me. A

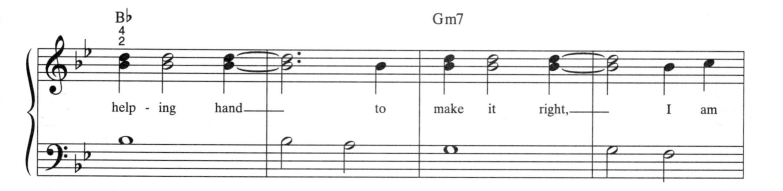

help - ing hand——— to make it right,——— I am

hold - ing you all through the night. I'll be the

98

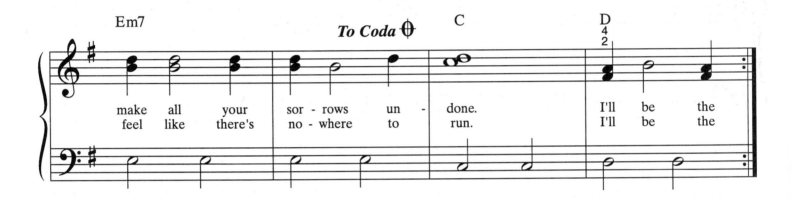

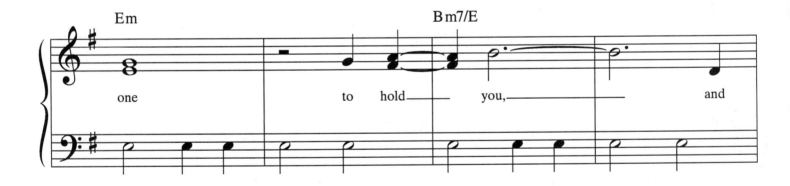

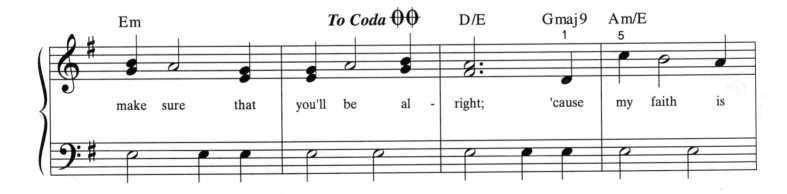

The One - 6 - 3

99

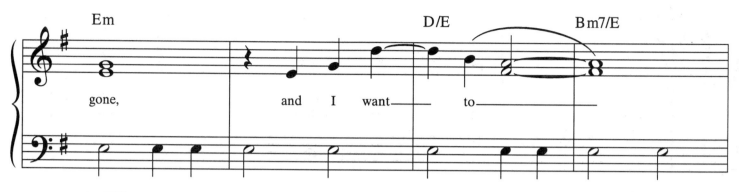

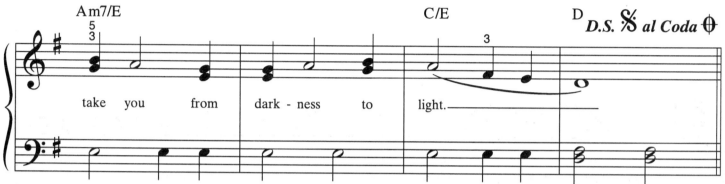

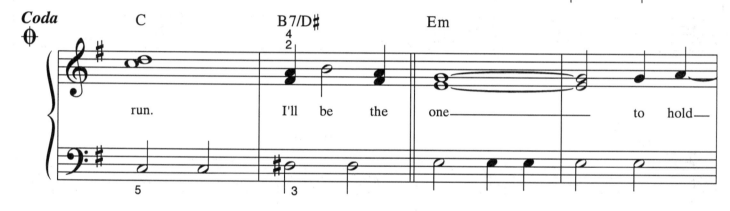

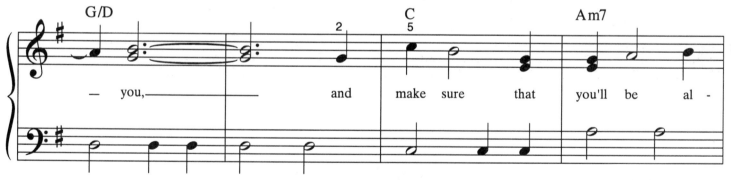

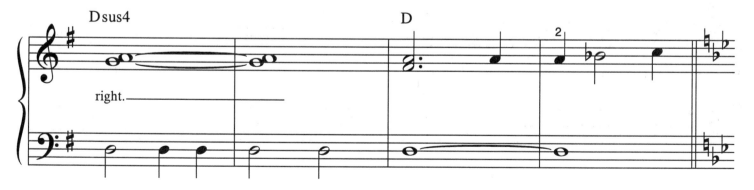

The One - 6 - 4

100

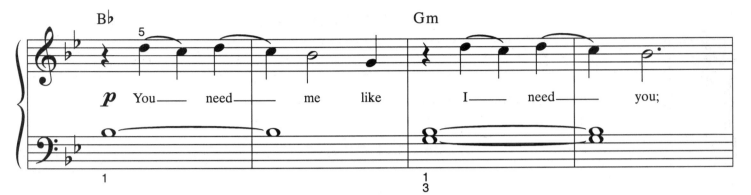

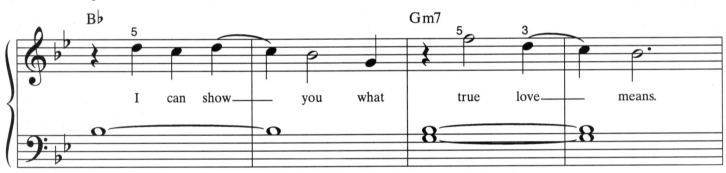

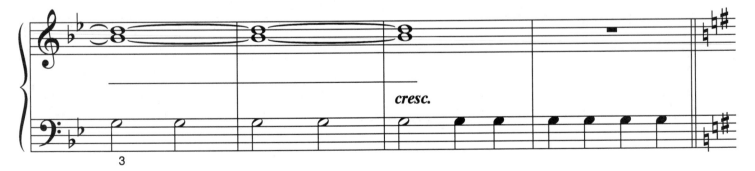

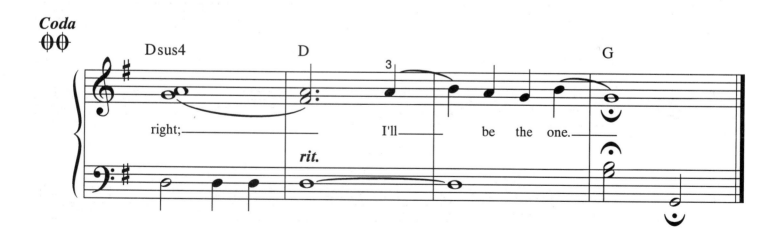

The One - 6 - 6

OOPS! ... I DID IT AGAIN

Words and Music by
MAX MARTIN and RAMI
Arranged by RICHARD BRADLEY

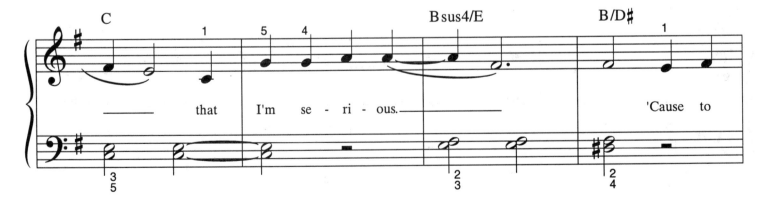

Oops! ... I Did It Again - 4 - 1

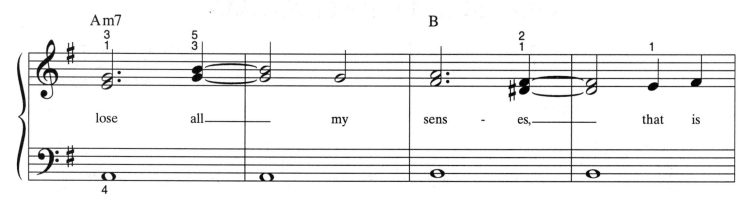

lose all_____ my sens - es,_____ that is

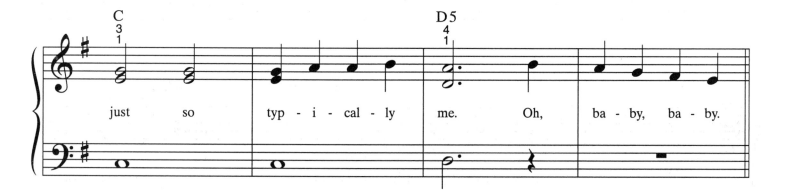

just so typ - i - cal - ly me. Oh, ba - by, ba - by.

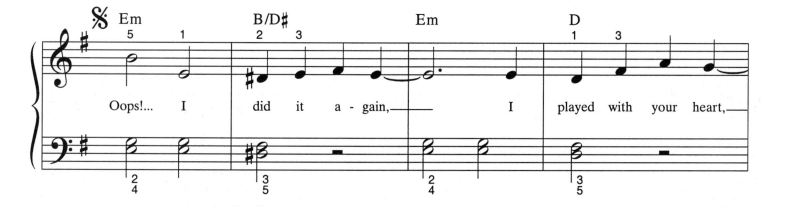

Oops!... I did it a - gain,_____ I played with your heart,_____

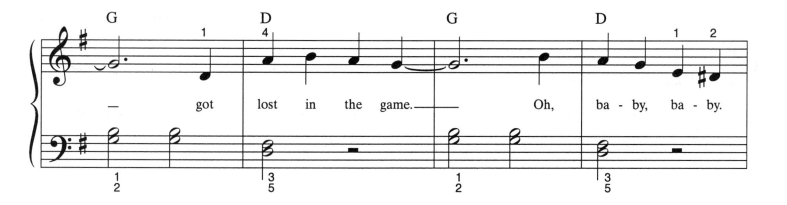

— got lost in the game._____ Oh, ba - by, ba - by.

104

To Coda

Oops!... You think I'm in love, that I'm sent from a - bove.

1.

I'm not that in - o - cent.

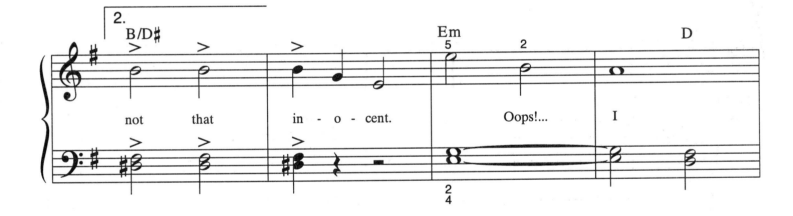

2.

not that in - o - cent. Oops!... I

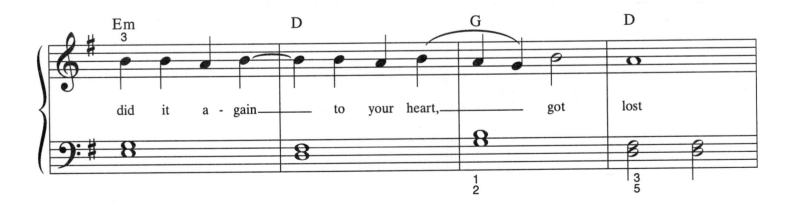

did it a - gain to your heart, got lost

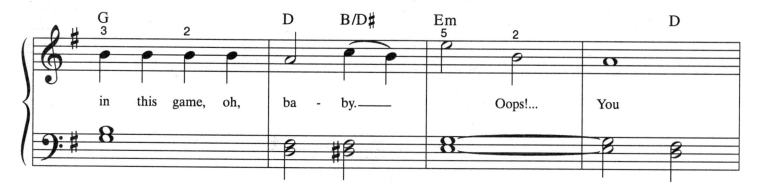

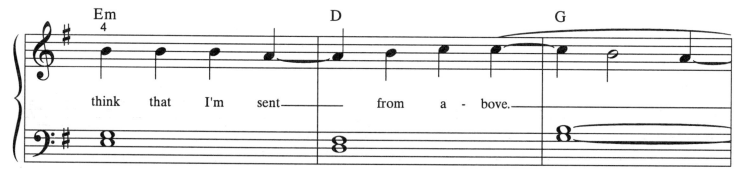

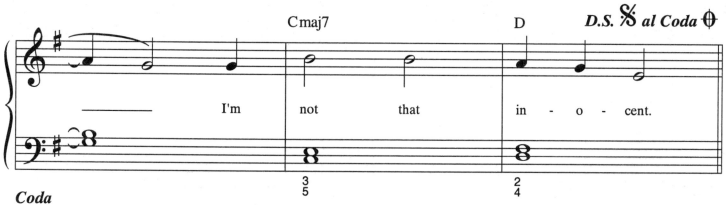

Verse 2:
You see my problem is this,
I'm dreaming away
Wishing that heroes, they truly exist.
I cry watching the days,
Can't you see I'm a fool, in so many ways?
But to . . .

Oops! ... I Did It Again - 4 - 4

PRIVATE EMOTION

Words and Music by
ROB HYMAN and ERIC BAZILIAN
Arranged by RICHARD BRADLEY

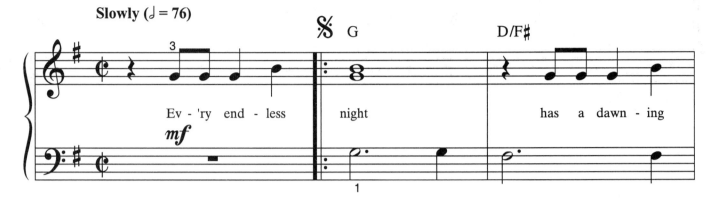

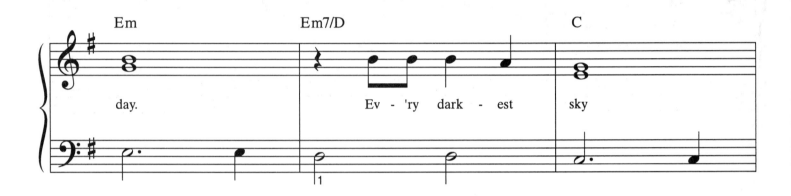

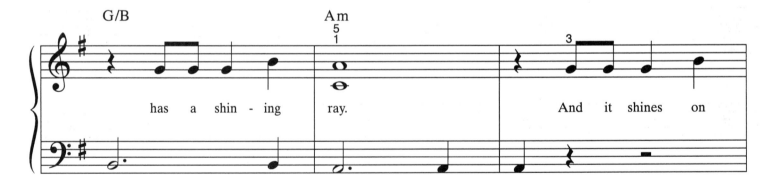

Private Emotion - 4 - 1

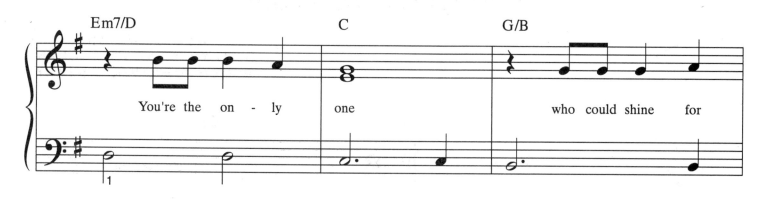

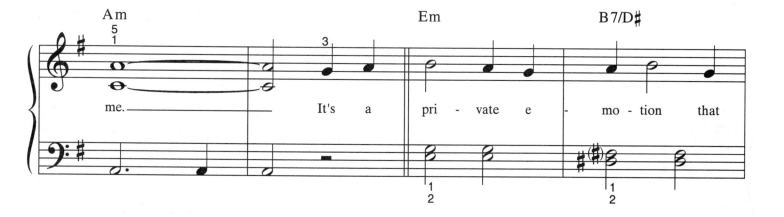

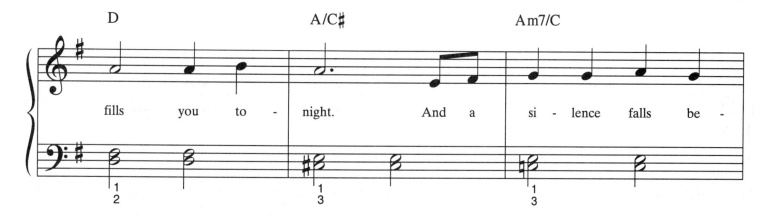

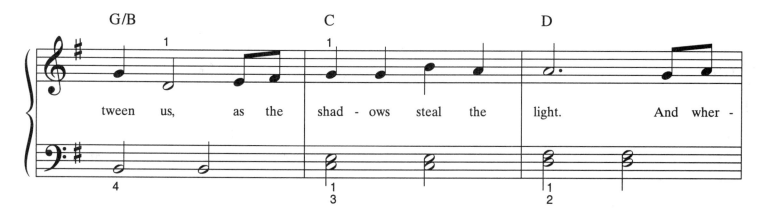

Private Emotion - 4 - 2

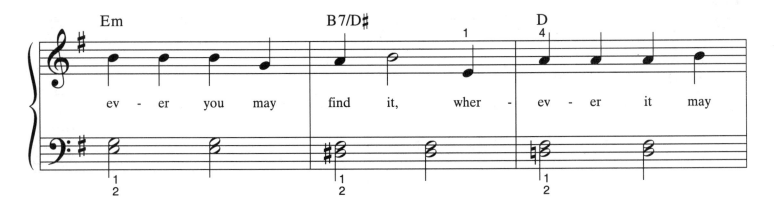

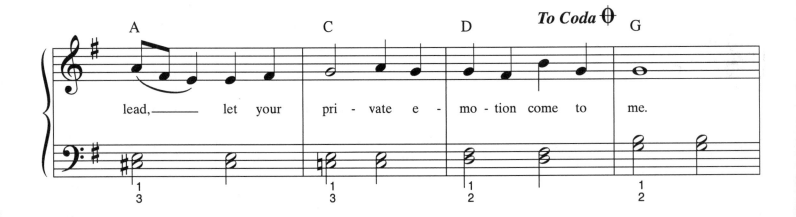

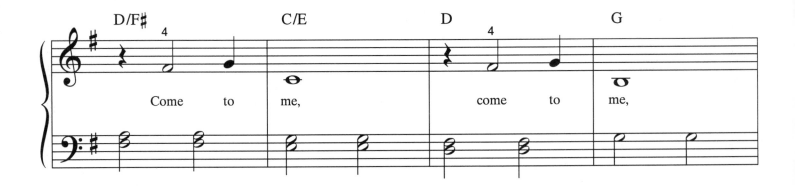

Coda

me.   Let your pri - vate e - mo - tion come to

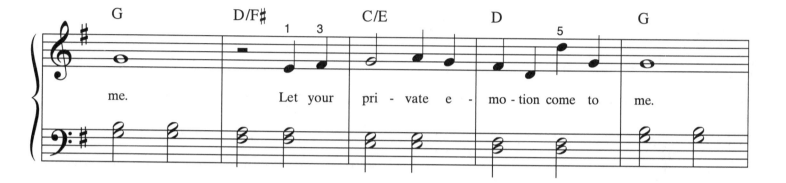

me.   Let your pri - vate e - mo - tion come to me.

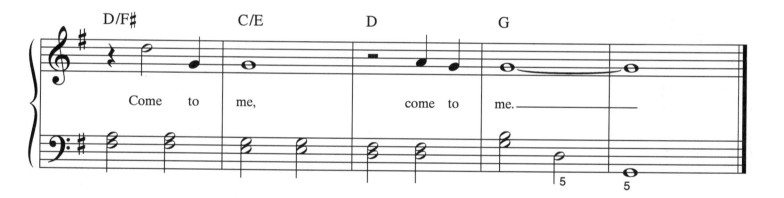

Come to me,   come to me. ———

Verse 2:
When your soul is tired and your heart is weak,
Do you think of love as a one-way street?
Well, it runs both ways. Open up your eyes,
Can't you see me here? How can you deny?
(To Chorus:)

Verse 3:
Every endless night has a dawning day.
Every darkest sky has a shinny ray.
It takes a lot to laugh as your tears go by.
But you can find me here till your tears run dry.
(To Chorus:)

SHOW ME THE MEANING OF BEING LONELY

Words and Music by
MAX MARTIN and **HERBERT CRICHLOW**
Arranged by **RICHARD BRADLEY**

Moderately slow (♩ = 92)

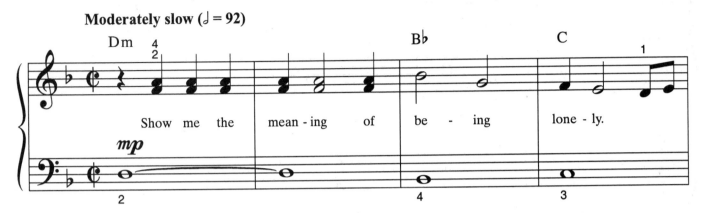

Show me the mean-ing of be-ing lone-ly.

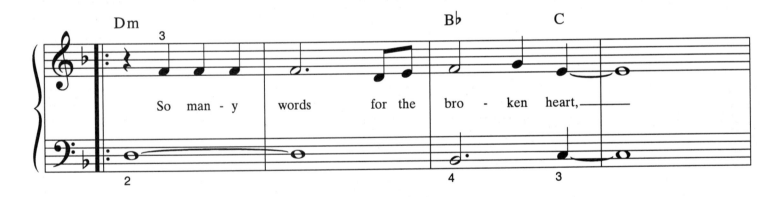

So man-y words for the bro-ken heart,

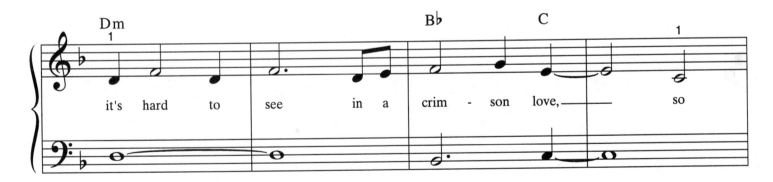

it's hard to see in a crim-son love, so

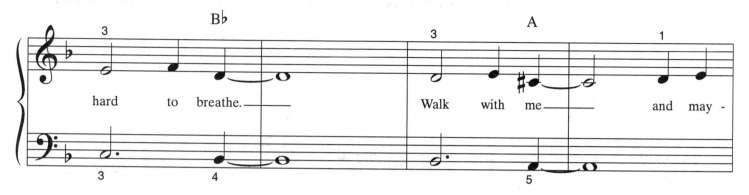

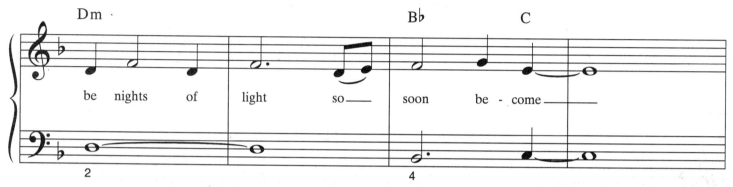

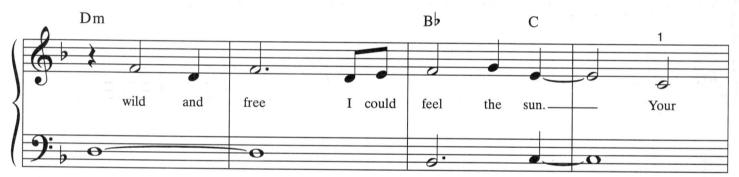

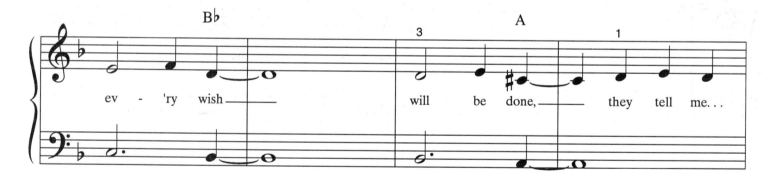

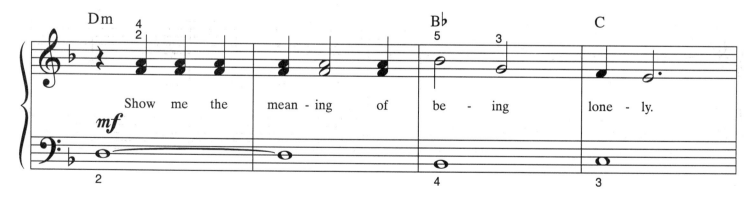

112

Is this the feel-ing I need to walk with?

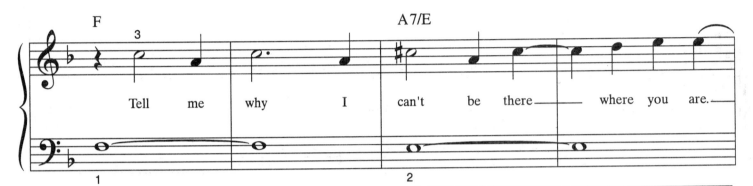

Tell me why I can't be there where you are.

1.
There's some-thing miss-ing in my heart.

2.
There's some-thing miss-ing in my

Show Me the Meaning of Being Lonely - 6 - 3

heart. There's no - where to run, I have no place to go.

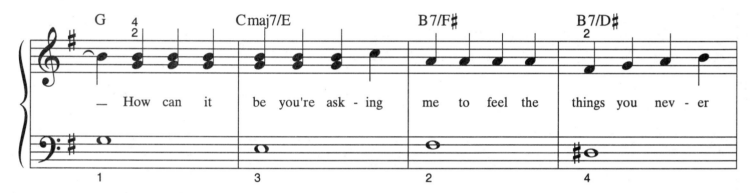

— Sur - ren - der my heart, bod - y and soul.

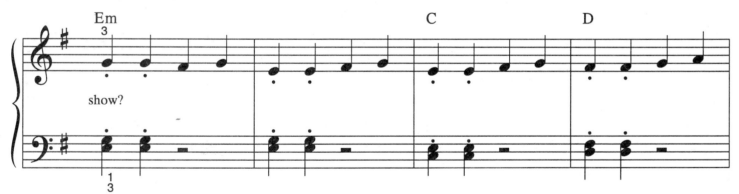

— How can it be you're ask - ing me to feel the things you nev - er

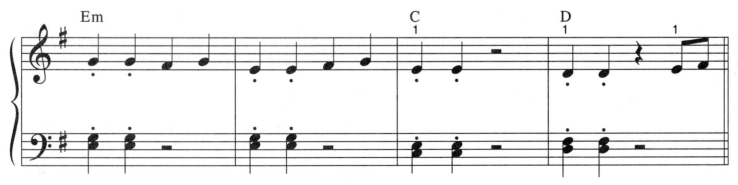

show?

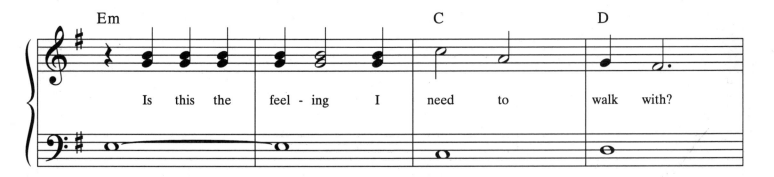

Is this the feel - ing I need to walk with?

Tell me why I can't be there where you are.

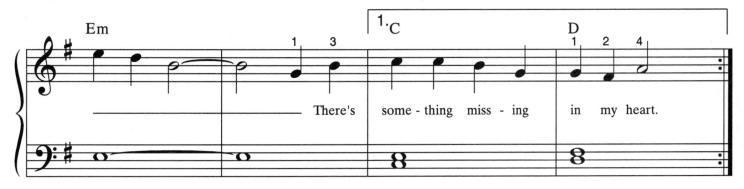

There's some - thing miss - ing in my heart.

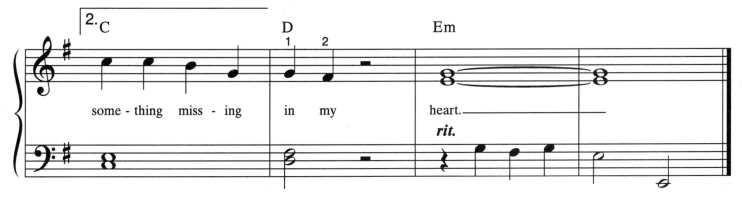

some - thing miss - ing in my heart.

rit.

Verse 2:
Life goes on as it never ends.
Eyes of stone observe the trends,
They never say, forever gaze.
If only guilty roads to an endless love,
There's no control. Are you with me now?
You're every wish will be done,
They tell me . . .
(To Chorus)

SMOOTH

Lyrics by ROB THOMAS
Music by ITAAL SHUR and ROB THOMAS
Arranged by RICHARD BRADLEY

Moderately (♩ = 228)

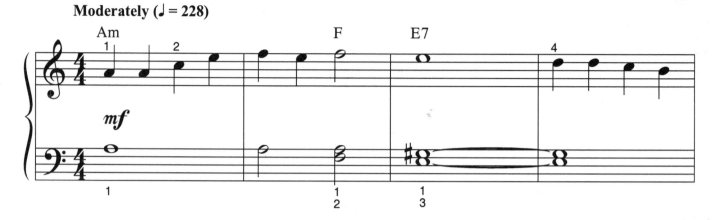

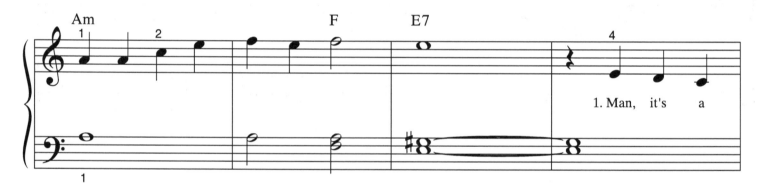

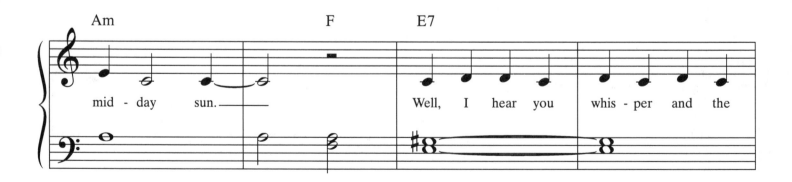

Smooth - 6 - 1

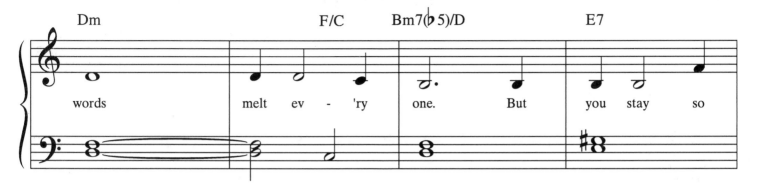

words — melt ev - 'ry one. But you stay so

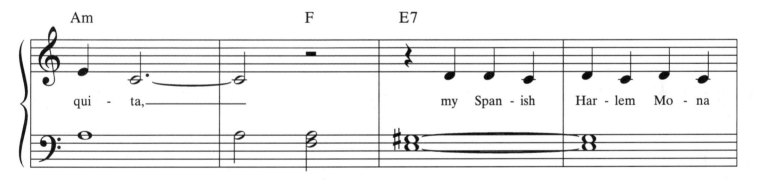

cool. — My mu - ñe -

qui - ta, — my Span - ish Har - lem Mo - na

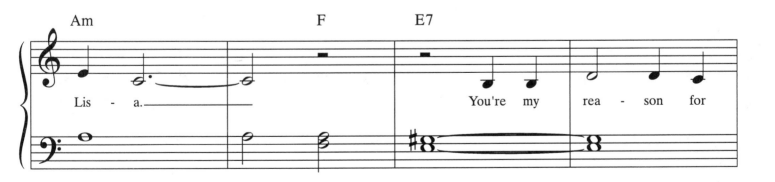

Lis - a. — You're my rea - son for

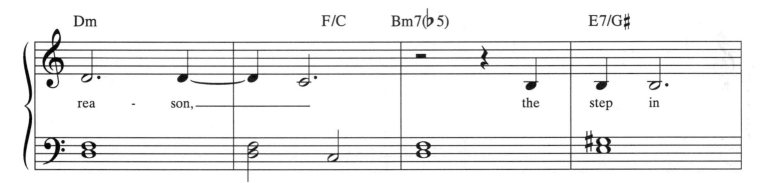

rea - son, the step in

my groove. And if you said

Pre-Chorus:

this life ain't good e-nough, I would give

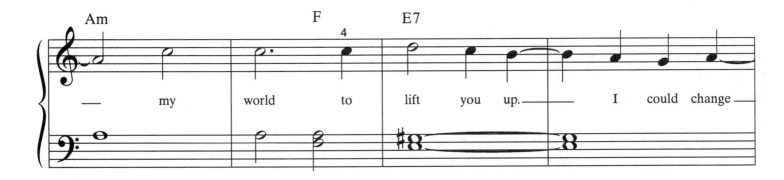

my world to lift you up. I could change

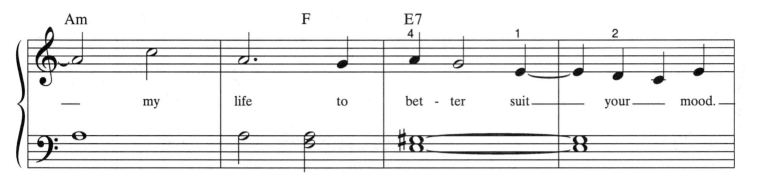

Am   F   E7

— my   life   to   bet - ter   suit _____ your _____ mood. _____

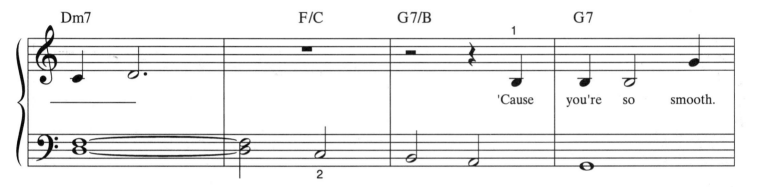

Dm7   F/C   G7/B   G7

_____   'Cause you're so smooth.

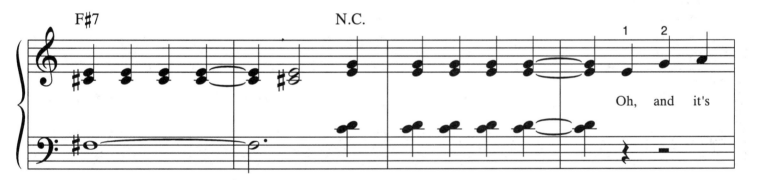

F#7   N.C.

Oh, and it's

Chorus:

Am   F   E7

just like the o - cean   un - derr the moon. _____ Well, it's the

same as the e - mo - tion that I get from you._____ You

got that kind of lov - ing that can be so smooth,_____ yeah.

1.

Give me your heart,____ make it real_____ or else for - get a - bout it.

2.

Give me your heart,____ make it real_____ or else for - get a - bout it.

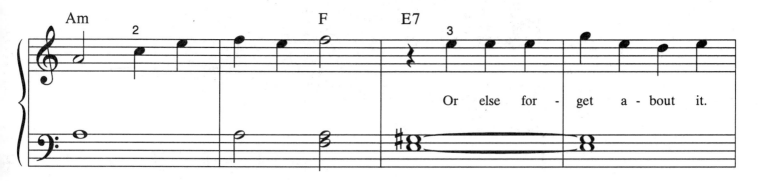

Or else for - get a - bout it.

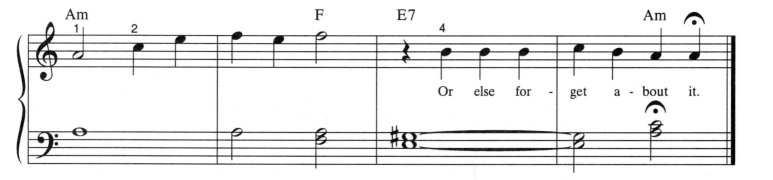

Or else for - get a - bout it.

Verse 2:
Well, I'll tell you one thing,
If you would leave, it be a crying shame.
In every breath and every word,
I hear your name calling me out, yeah.
Well, out from the barrio,
You hear my rhythm on your radio.
You feel the tugging of the world,
So soft and slow, turning you 'round and 'round.

From the Motion Picture *DOGMA*

STILL

Words and Music by
ALANIS MORISSETTE
Arranged by RICHARD BRADLEY

Slowly (♩ = 74)

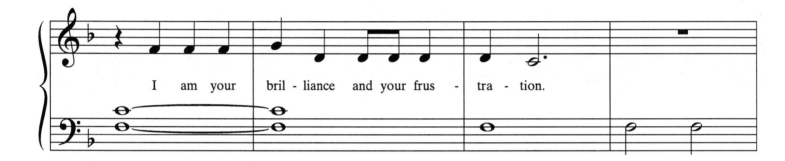

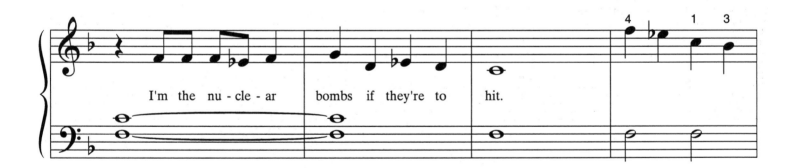

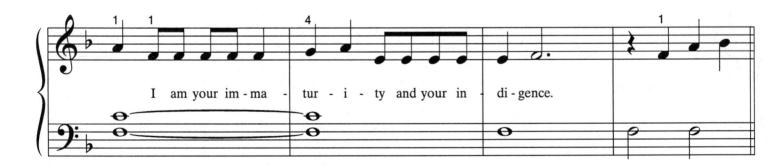

Still - 4 - 1

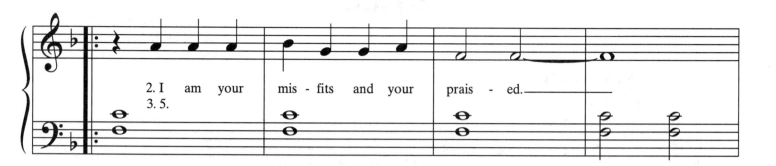

2. I am your mis - fits and your prais - ed.
3. 5.

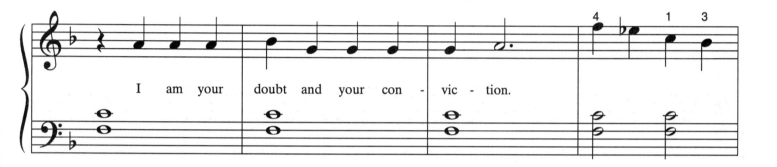

I am your doubt and your con - vic - tion.

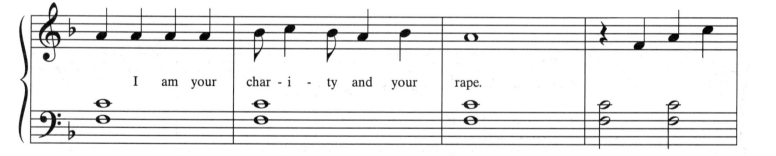

I am your char - i - ty and your rape.

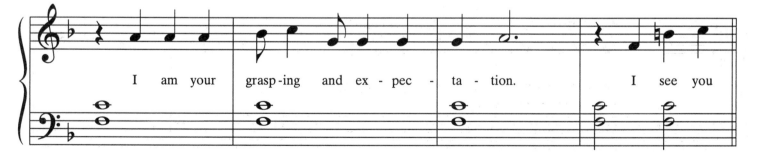

I am your grasp - ing and ex - pec - ta - tion. I see you

124

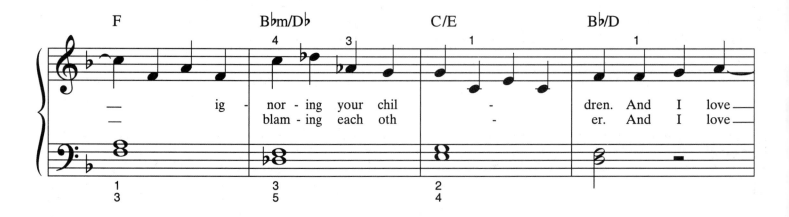

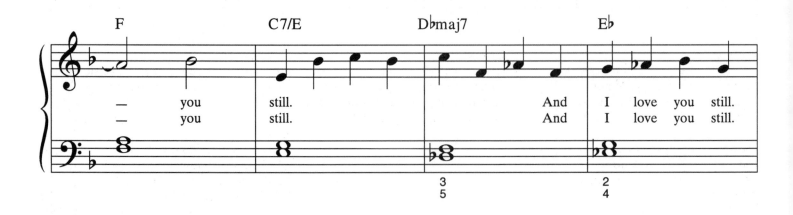

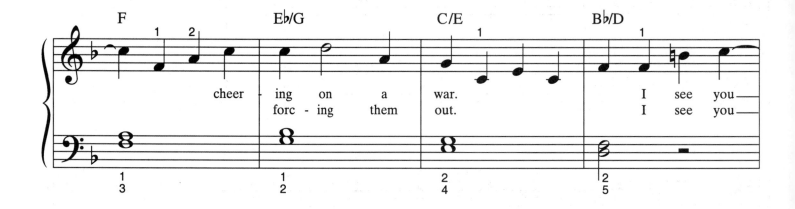

Still - 4 - 3

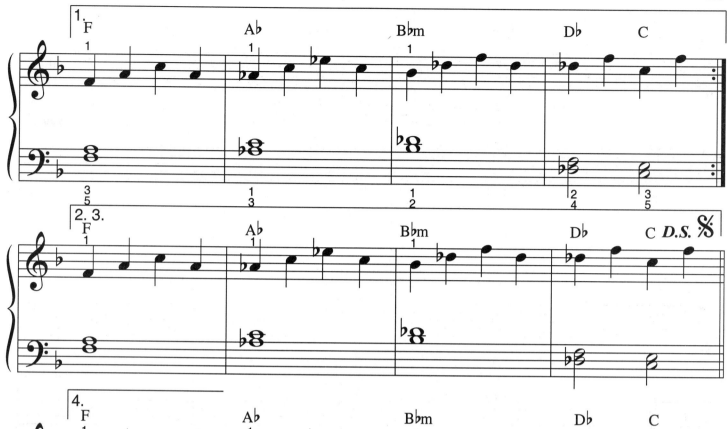

Verse 3:
I am your misfits and your praised.
I am your fury and your elation.
I am your yearning and your sweat.
I am your faithless and your religion.

I see you altering history.
I see you abusing the land.
I see you and your selective amnesia.
And I love you still.

Verse 4:
I am your tragedy and your fortune.
I am your crisis and your delight.
I am your prophets and your profits.
I am your art, I am your bytes.

Verse 5:
I am your death and your decisioins.
I am your passion and your plights.
I am your sickness and convalescence.
I am your weapons and your light.

I see you holding your grudges.
I see you gunning them down.
I see you silencing your sisters.
And I love you still.

STOP (ASÍ)

Words and Music by
EMILIO ESTEFAN, JR., JON SECADA,
GEORGE NORIEGA and TIM MITCHELL
Arranged by RICHARD BRADLEY

Moderately (♩ = 100)

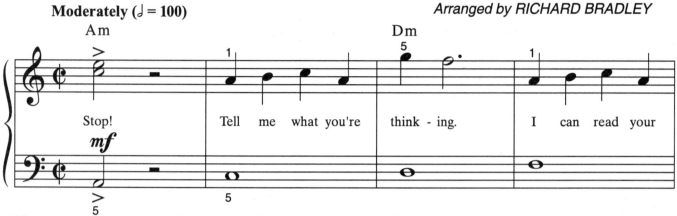

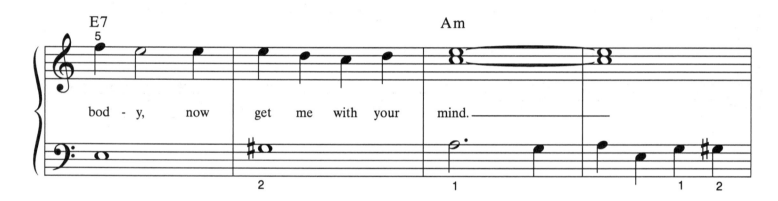

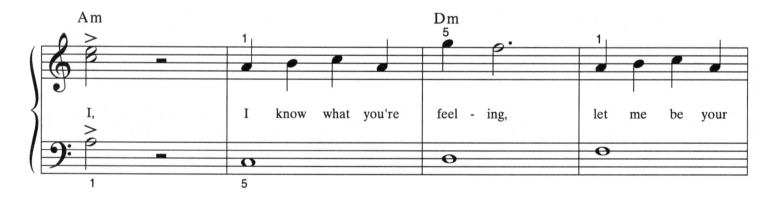

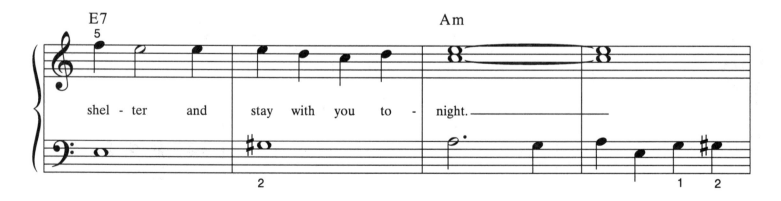

Stop (Así) - 4 - 1

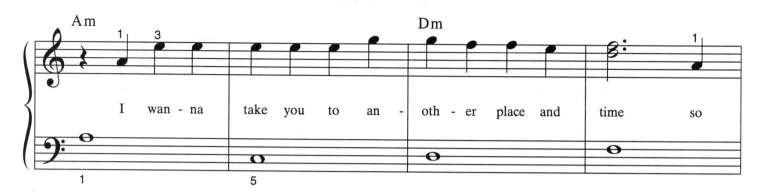

I wan - na take you to an - oth - er place and time so

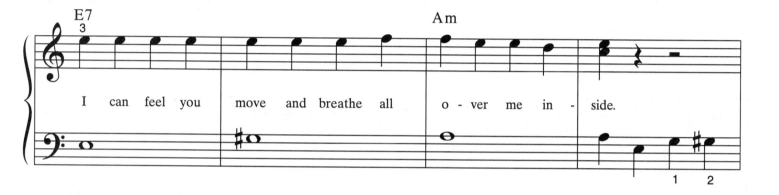

I can feel you move and breathe all o - ver me in - side.

Don't be a - fraid to tell me how you want to feel. Just

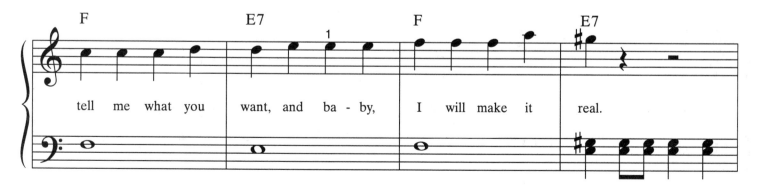

tell me what you want, and ba - by, I will make it real.

Stop (Así) - 4 - 2

Stop!   Tell   me   what   you're

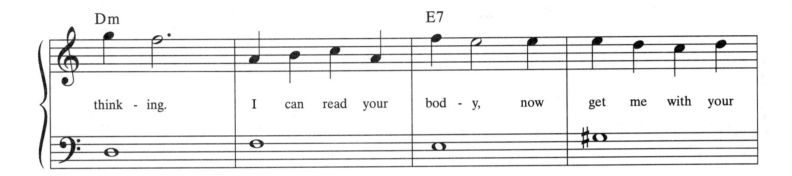

think - ing.   I   can   read   your   bod - y,   now   get   me   with   your

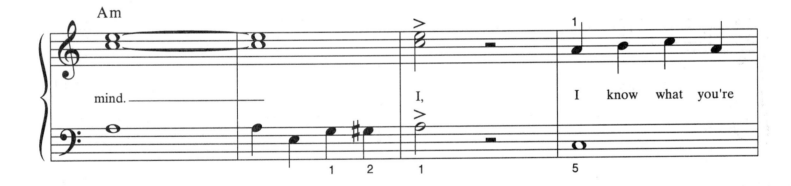

mind. _____   I,   I   know   what   you're

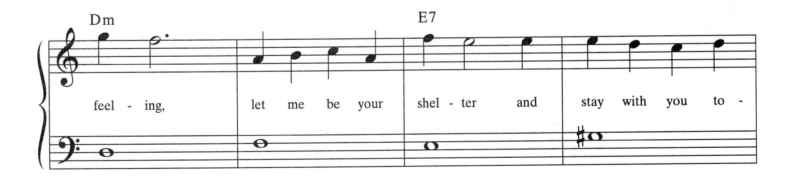

feel - ing,   let   me   be   your   shel - ter   and   stay   with   you   to -

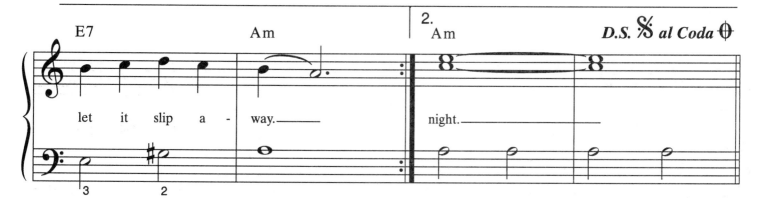

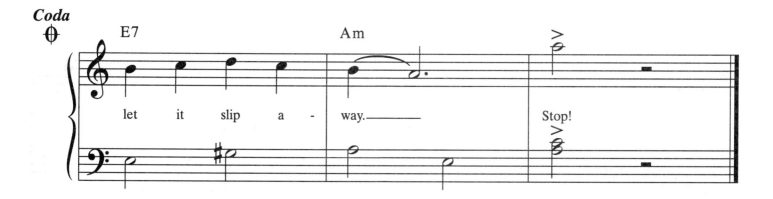

THAT'S THE WAY IT IS

Words and Music by
MAX MARTIN, KRISTIAN LUNDIN
and ANDREAS CARLSSON
Arranged by RICHARD BRADLEY

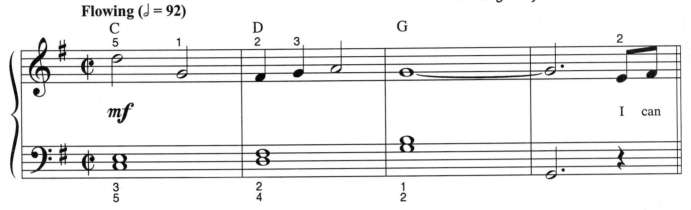

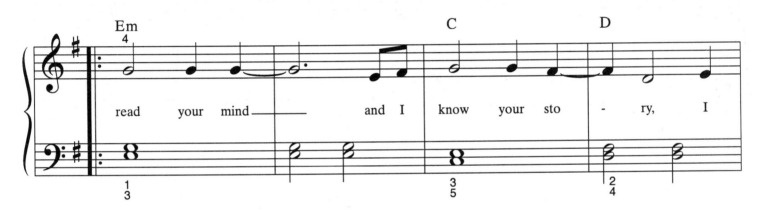

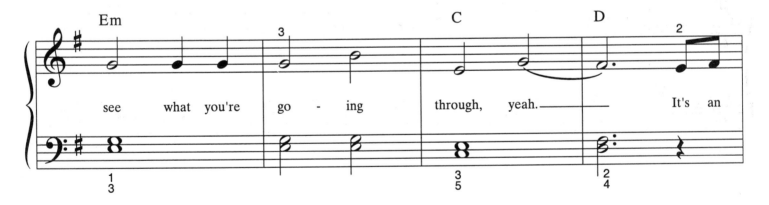

That's the Way It Is - 6 - 1

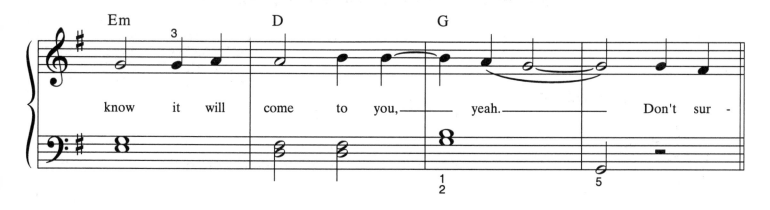

know it will come to you,————— yeah.————————— Don't sur -

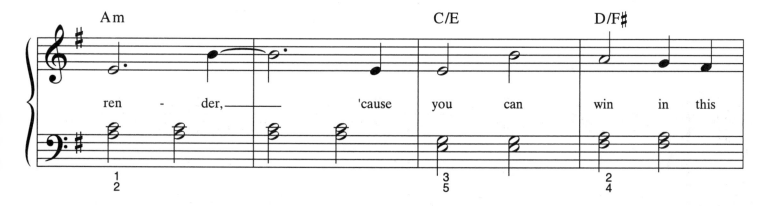

ren - der,———————— 'cause you can win in this

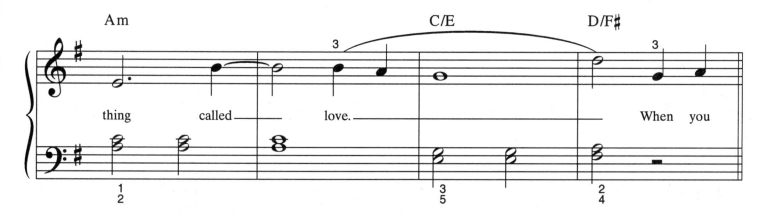

thing called———— love.——————————————— When you

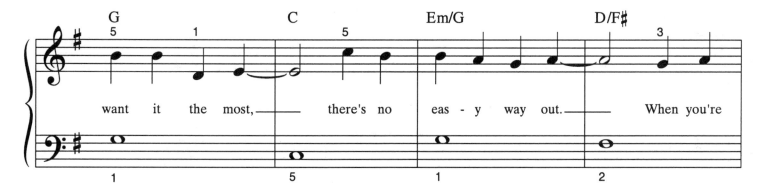

want it the most,———— there's no eas - y way out.———— When you're

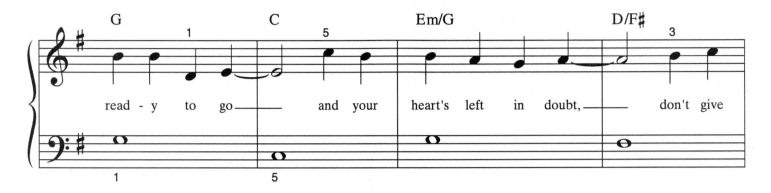

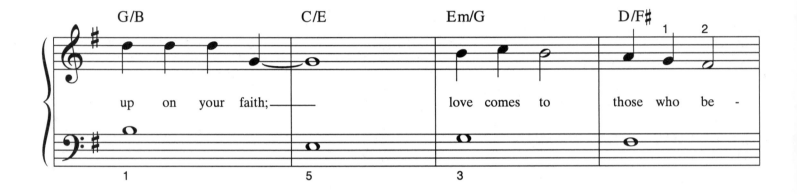

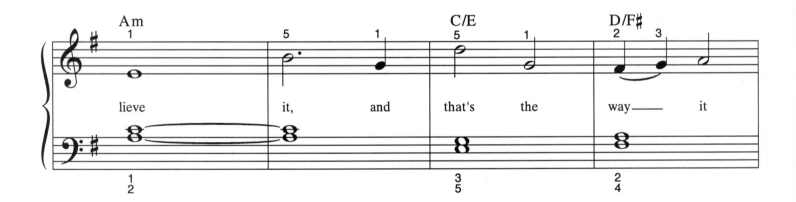

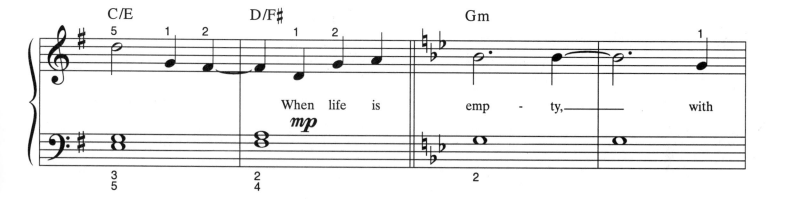

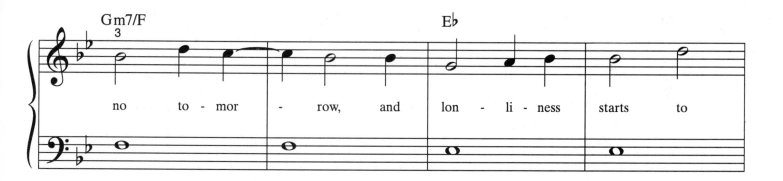

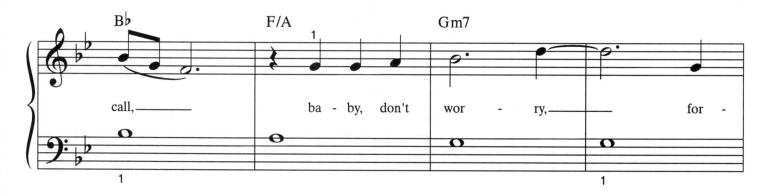

That's the Way It Is - 6 - 4

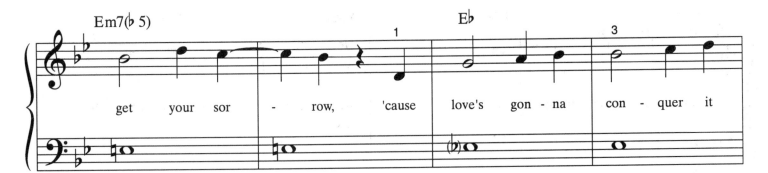

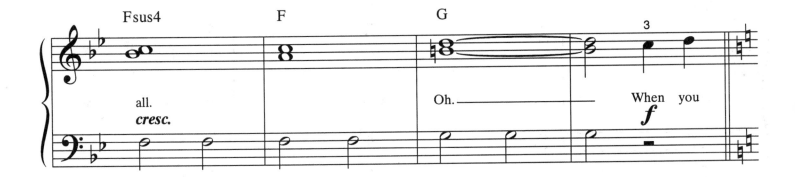

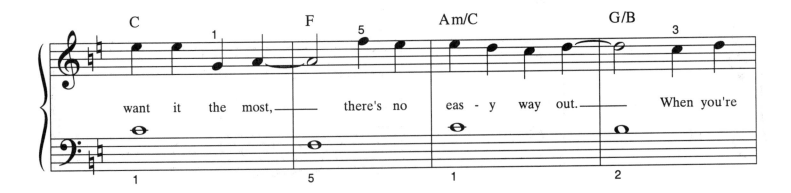

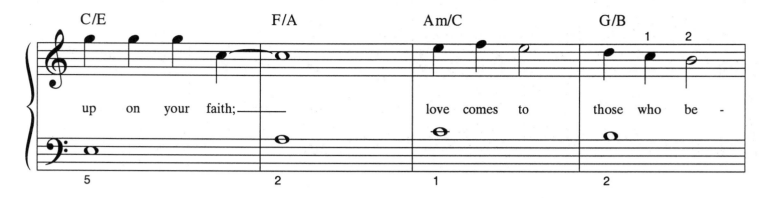

up on your faith;_____ love comes to those who be -

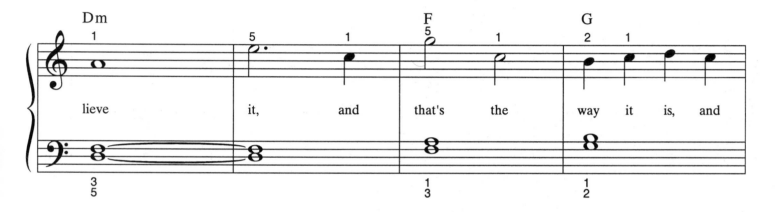

lieve it, and that's the way it is, and

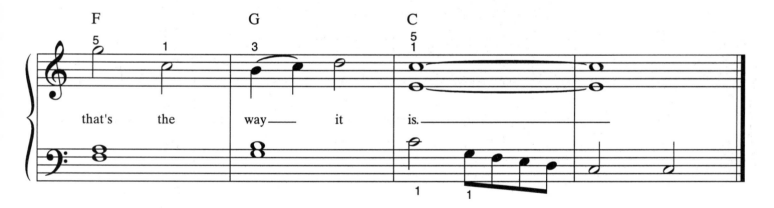

that's the way___ it is._____

Verse 2:
When you question me for a simple answer,
I don't know what to say, no.
But it's plain to see, if you stick together,
You're gonna find the way, yeah.

SWEAR IT AGAIN

Words and Music by
STEVE MAC and WAYNE HECTOR
Arranged by RICHARD BRADLEY

Moderately (♩ = 65)

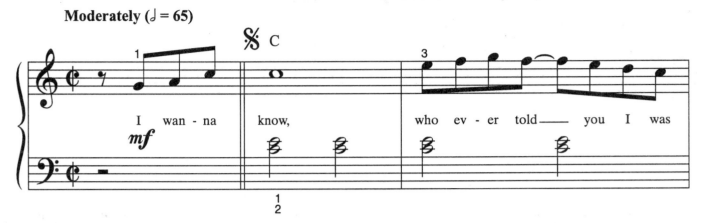

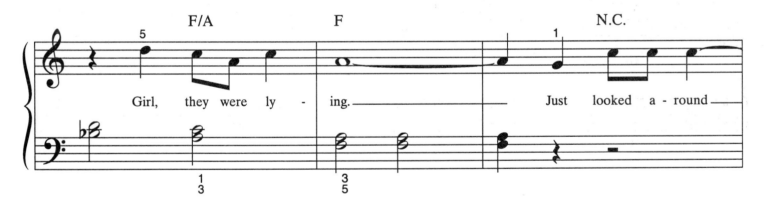

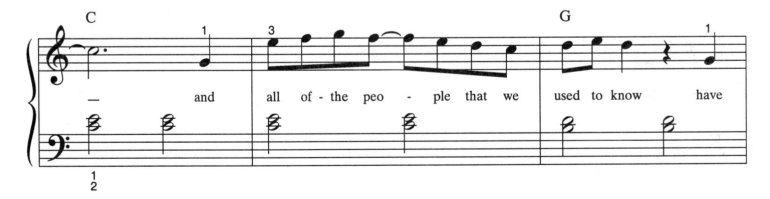

Swear It Again - 5 - 1

just giv - en up,——— they wan - na let it go, but we're still

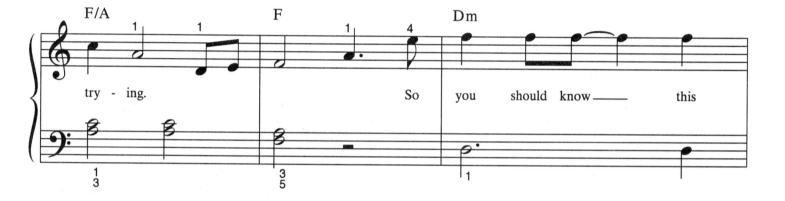

try - ing. So you should know——— this

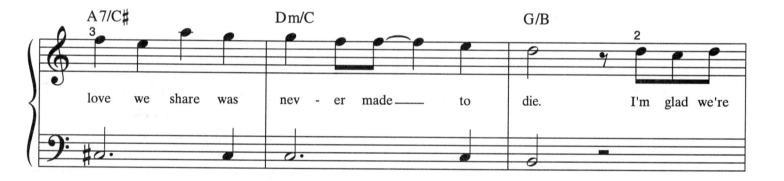

love we share was nev - er made——— to die. I'm glad we're

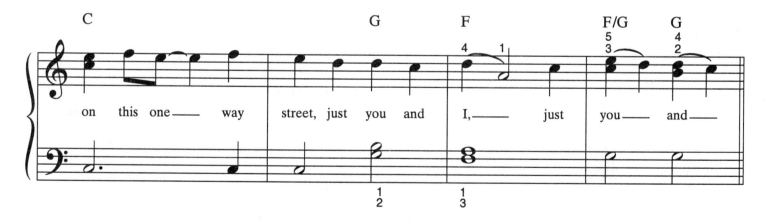

on this one——— way street, just you and I,——— just you——— and———

138

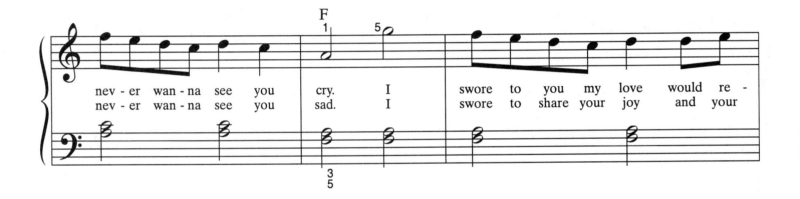

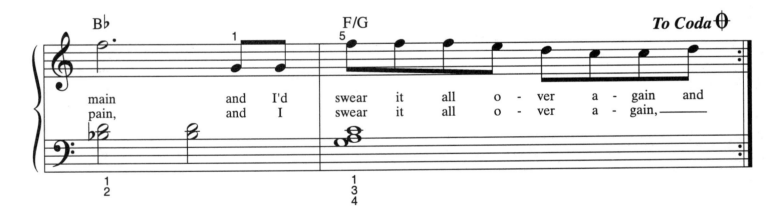

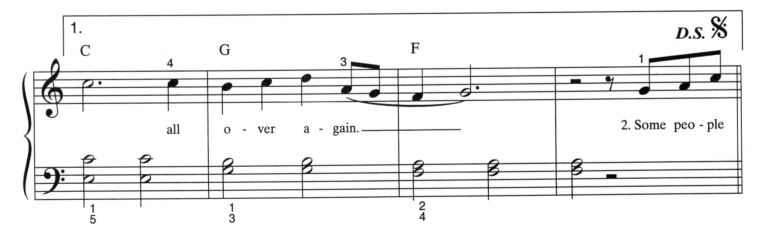

Swear It Again - 5 - 3

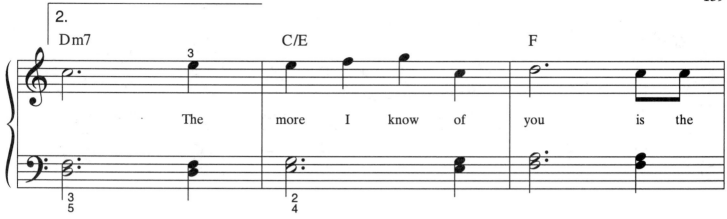

2.

The more I know of you is the

more I know —— I love you, and the more that I'm sure ——

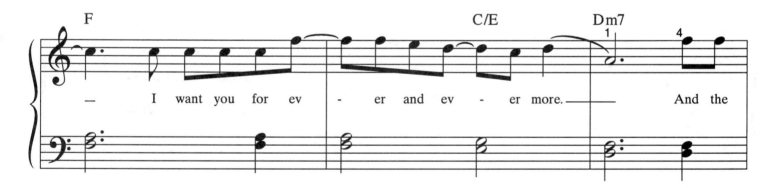

— I want you for ev - er and ev - er more. —— And the

more that you love me, the more that I know, ——

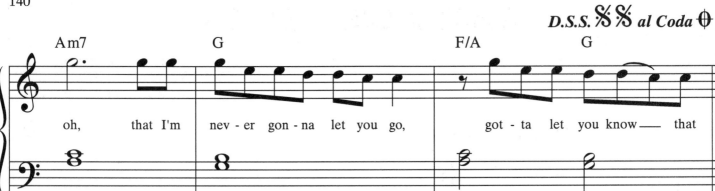

oh,   that I'm   nev - er gon - na let you go,   got - ta let you know ___ that

Coda ⊕

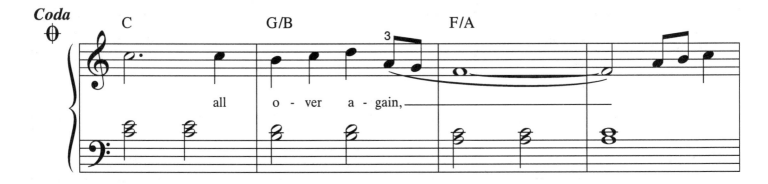

all   o - ver a - gain, ___

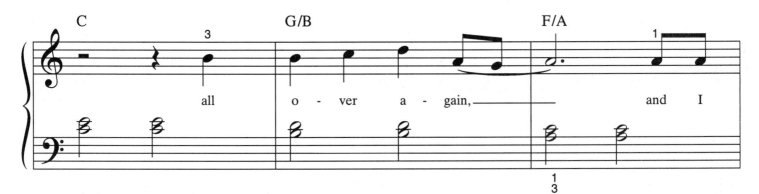

all   o - ver a - gain, ___   and I

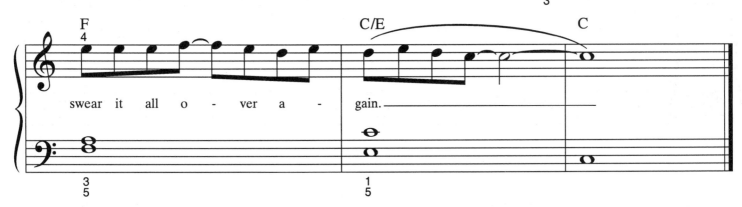

swear it all o - ver a - gain. ___

Verse 2:
Some people say, that everything has got its place and time,
Even the day must give way to the night, but I'm not buying.
'Cause in your eyes I see a love that burns eternally,
And if you see how beautiful you are to me, you'll know I'm not lying.
Sure, there'll be times we wanna say good-bye, but even if we tried,
There are some things in this life won't be denied, won't be denied.

WHAT A GIRL WANTS

Words and Music by
GUY ROCHE and SHELLY PEIKEN
Arranged by Richard Bradley

Slow, funky groove (♩ = 72)

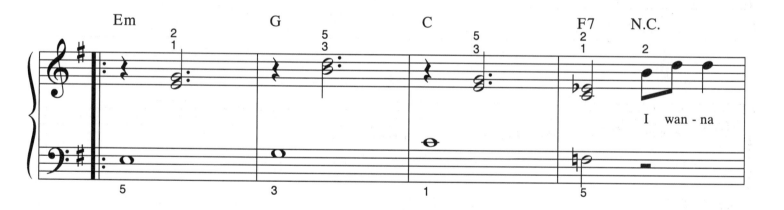

What a Girl Wants - 5 - 1

142

ed so___ pa-tient-ly___ while I got it to-geth-er, hmm,

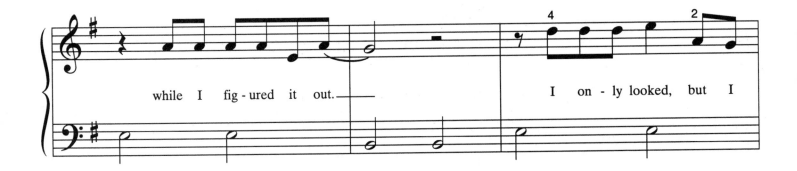

while I fig-ured it out.___ I on-ly looked, but I

nev-er touched___ 'cause in my heart___ was a pic-ture of us

Am7   C/D

hold-in' hands,___ mak-in' plans, and it's luck-y for me___ you un-

What a Girl Wants - 5 - 2

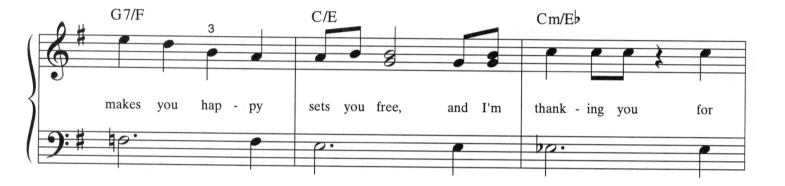

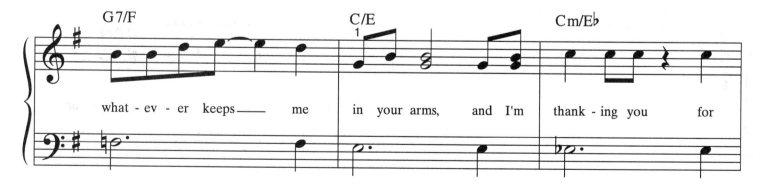

What a Girl Wants - 5 - 3

144

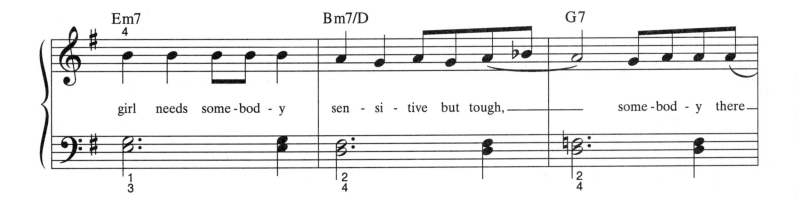

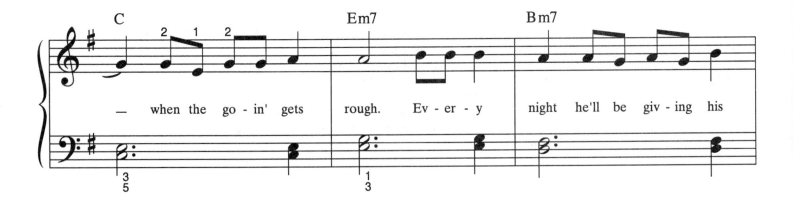

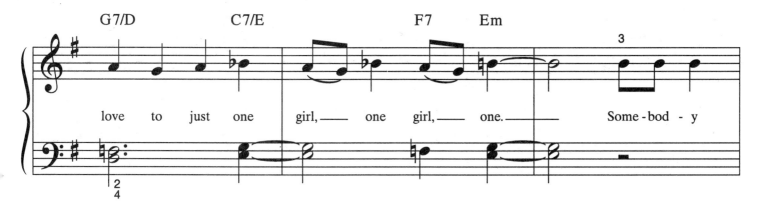

love to just one girl, ___ one girl, ___ one. ___ Some-bod-y

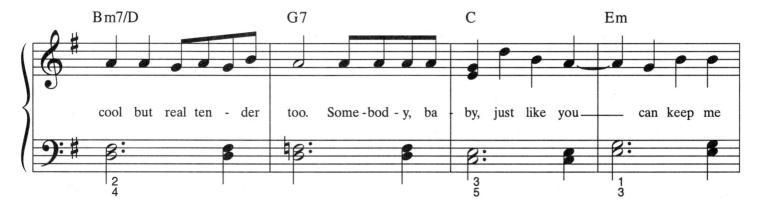

cool but real ten-der too. Some-bod-y, ba-by, just like you ___ can keep me

D.S. 𝄋 **and Fade**

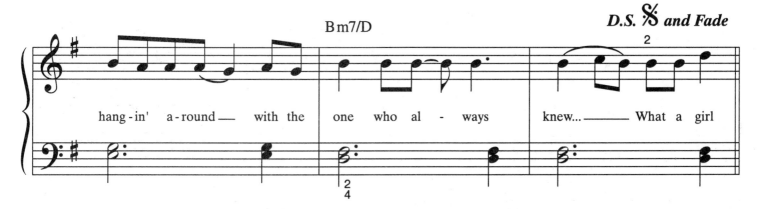

hang-in' a-round ___ with the one who al-ways knew... ___ What a girl

Verse 2:
A weaker man might have walked away, but you had faith,
Strong enough to move over and give me space
While I got it together, while I figured it out.
They say if you love something, let it go;
If it comes back, it's yours.
That's how you know it's for keeps, yeah, it's for sure,
And you're ready and willin' to give me more than . . .
(To Chorus:)

As Long As You Love Me

By
MAX MARTIN
Arranged by RICHARD BRADLEY

Moderate (♩ = 100)

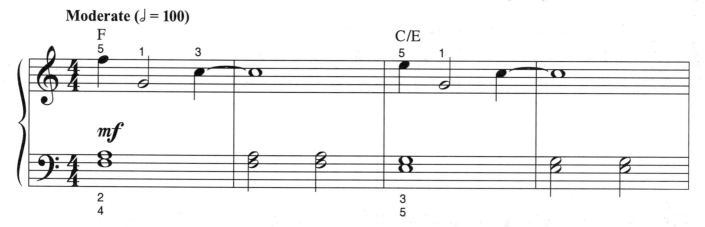

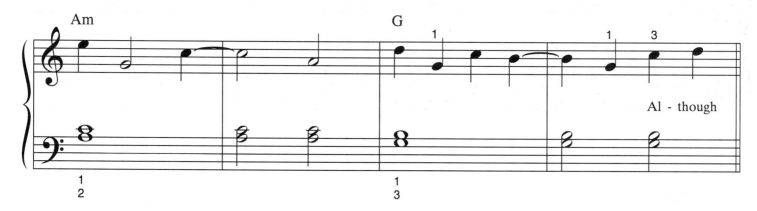

Al - though

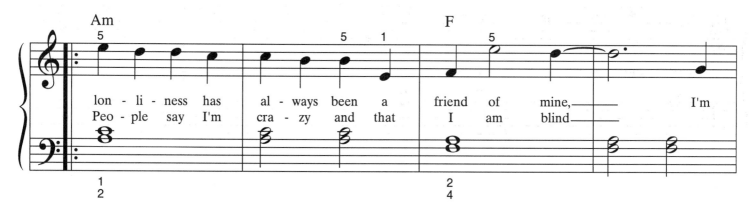

lon - li - ness has | al - ways been a | friend of mine,_____ | I'm
Peo - ple say I'm | cra - zy and that | I am blind_____ | I'm

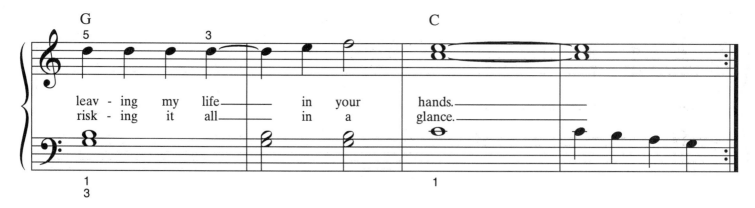

leav - ing my life_____ | in your | hands._____ |
risk - ing it all | in a | glance. |

As Long As You Love Me - 6 - 1

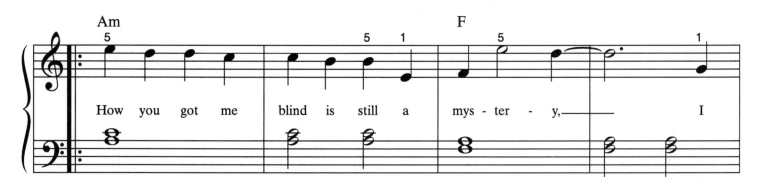

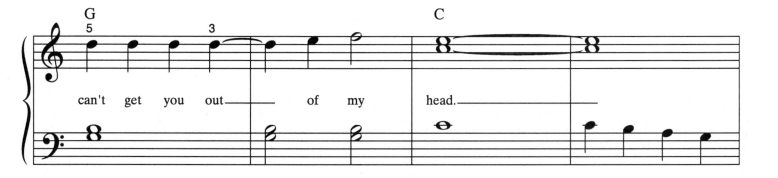

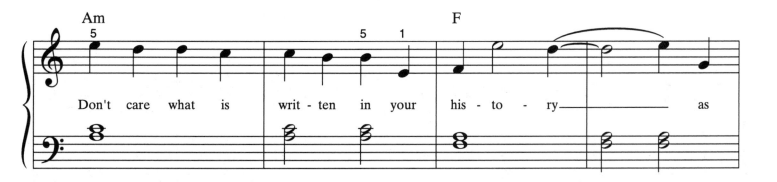

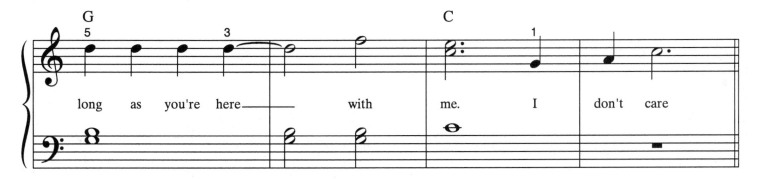

148

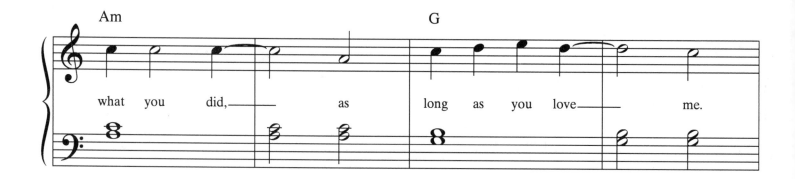

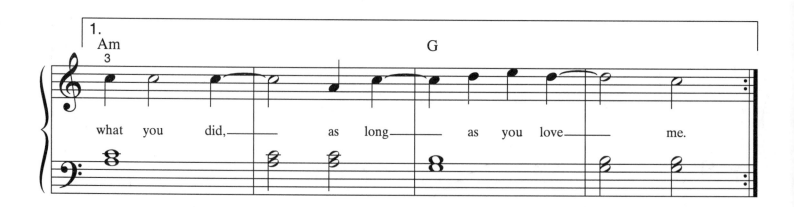

As Long As You Love Me - 6 - 3

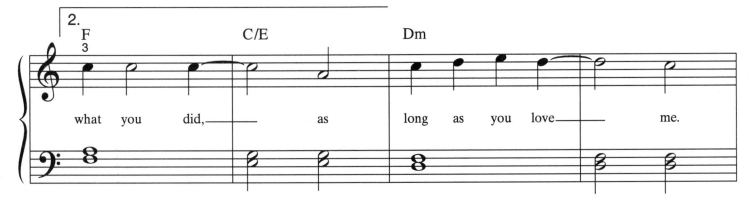

what you did,_____ as long as you love_____ me.

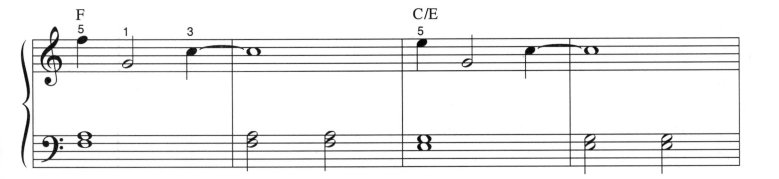

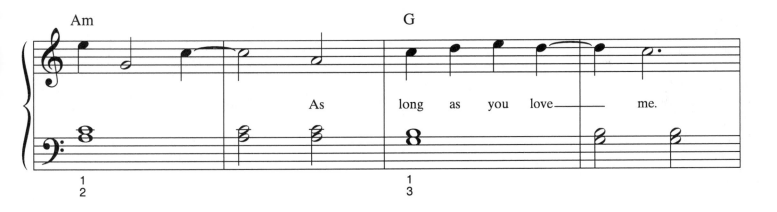

As long as you love_____ me.

As Long As You Love Me - 6 - 4

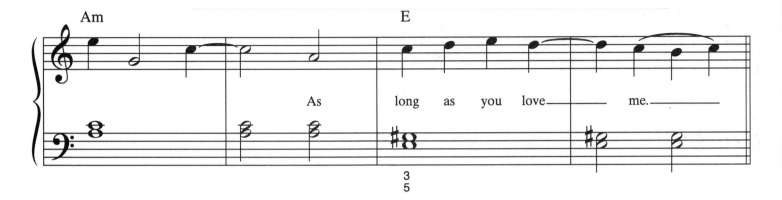

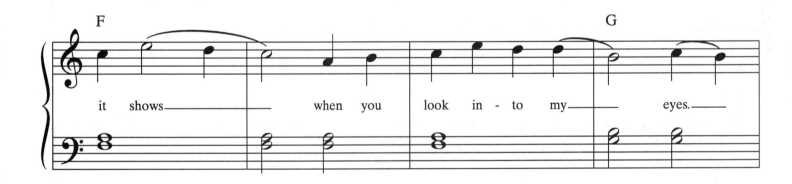

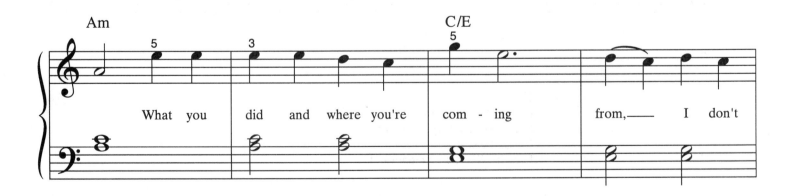

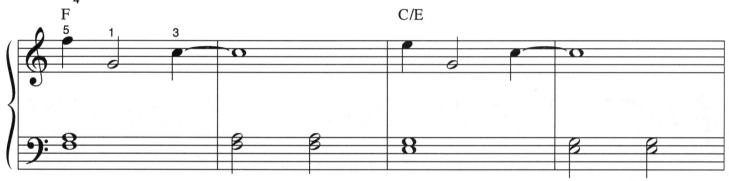

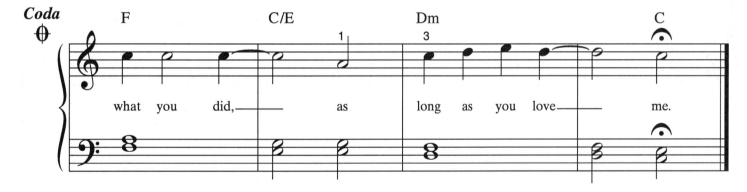

Verse 3:
Every little thing that you have said and done
Feels like it's deep within me.
Doesn't really matter if you're on the run,
It seems like we're meant to be.

RICHARD BRADLEY

Richard Bradley is one of the world's best-known and best-selling arrangers of piano music for print. His success can be attributed to years of experience as a teacher and his understanding of students' and players' needs. His innovative piano methods for adults (*Bradley's How to Play Piano* – Adult Books 1, 2, and 3) and kids (*Bradley for Kids* – Red, Blue, and Green Series) not only teach the instrument, but they also teach musicanship each step of the way.

Originally from the Chicago area, Richard completed his undergraduate and graduate work at the Chicago Conservatory of Music and Roosevelt University. After college, Richard became a print arranger for Hansen Publications and later became music director of Columbia Pictures Publications. In 1977, he co-founded his own publishing company, Bradley Publications, which is now exclusively distributed worldwide by Warner Bros. Publications.

Richard is equally well known for his piano workshops, clinics, and teacher training seminars. He was a panelist for the first and second Keyboard Teachers' National Video Conferences, which were attended by more than 20,000 piano teachers throughout the United States.

The home video version of his adult teaching method, *How to Play Piano With Richard Bradley*, was nominated for an American Video Award as Best Music Instruction Video, and, with sales climbing each year since its release, it has brought thousands of adults to—or back to—piano lessons. Still, Richard advises, "The video can only get an adult started and show them what they can do. As they advance, all students need direct input from an accomplished teacher."

Additional Richard Bradley videos aimed at other than the beginning pianist include *How to Play Blues Piano* and *How to Play Jazz Piano*. As a frequent television talk show guest on the subject of music education, Richard's many appearances include "Hour Magazine" with Gary Collins, "The Today Show," and "Mother's Day" with former "Good Morning America" host Joan Lunden, as well as dozens of local shows.